MULTICULTURAL FOUN
PSYCHOLOGY AND CC
Series Editors: Allen E. Ivey and

MW00563662

Counseling and Psychotherapy with Arabs and Muslims:
A Culturally Sensitive Approach
Marwan Dwairy

Healing the Soul Wound:
Counseling with American Indians and Other Native Peoples
Eduardo Duran

Learning from My Mother's Voice:
Family Legend and the Chinese American Experience
Jean Lau Chin

Community Genograms:
Using Individual, Family, and Cultural Narratives with Clients
Sandra A. Rigazio-DiGilio, Allen E. Ivey,
Kara P. Kunkler-Peck, and Lois T. Grady

Multicultural Encounters:
Case Narratives from a Counseling Practice
Stephen Murphy-Shigematsu

COUNSELING
and
PSYCHOTHERAPY
with
ARABS *and* MUSLIMS

A Culturally Sensitive Approach

MARWAN DWAIRY

FOREWORD BY PAUL B. PEDERSEN

Teachers College, Columbia University
New York and London

Published by Teachers College Press, 1234 Amsterdam Avenue, New York, NY 10027

Copyright © 2006 by Teachers College, Columbia University

All rights reserved. No part of this publication may be reproduced or transmitted in any form or by any means, electronic or mechanical, including photocopy, or any information storage and retrieval system, without permission from the publisher.

Library of Congress Cataloging-in-Publication Data

Dwairy, Marwan Adeeb.
  Counseling and psychotherapy with Arabs and Muslims : a culturally sensitive approach / Marwan Dwairy ; foreword by Paul B. Pedersen.
    p. cm. — (Multicultural foundations of psychology and counseling)
  Includes bibliographical references and index.
  ISBN-13: 978-0-8077-4701-8 (cloth)
  ISBN-10: 0-8077-4701-7 (cloth)
  ISBN-13: 978-0-8077-4700-1 (pbk. : alk. paper)
  ISBN-10: 0-8077-4700-9 (pbk. : alk. paper)
      1. Cross-cultural counseling.   2. Psychotherapy.   3. Palestinian Arabs—Counseling of.   4. Palestinian Arabs—Psychology.   5. Muslims—Counseling of.   6. Muslims—Psychology.
  BF637.C6D84 2006
  158′.3089927—dc22   2005055972

ISBN 13: 978-0-8077-4700-1 (paper)   ISBN 10: 0-8077-4700-9 (paper)
ISBN 13: 978-0-8077-4701-8 (cloth)   ISBN 10: 0-8077-4701-7 (cloth)

Printed on acid-free paper
Manufactured in the United States of America

13   12   11   10   09   08   07   06   8   7   6   5   4   3   2   1

Contents

Foreword

When I finished reading Marwan Dwairy's 1998 book *Cross-Cultural Counseling,* I immediately sent an order for five copies to the publishers for me to give away. This new book, which promises to have an equally powerful effect, is important for several reasons. First, it brings a message that you will not read in any of the current textbooks about specific cultural bias in the counseling profession. Second, it provides a plan for reframing the counseling process to fit the needs of a collectivistic society, which describes the majority of the world's people, and demonstrates the dangers of imposed individualism. Third, it provides practical suggestions and advice for "low context" counselors communicating with "high context" clients building on historical traditions. Fourth, it deals directly with the consequences of simplistic stereotyping of Arabic and Muslim people following the September 11 events and the threat of terrorism. Fifth, it introduces a new methodology in counseling of a "biopsychosocial" model and the use of metaphors in counseling.

The book is divided into three sections, making it easier for the reader to make a transition from one topic to the next. The first section looks at heritage and historical context so that the reader can better understand the development of ideas from their source. The second section is about development and personality patterns that again help the reader better understand both the similarities and differences between the Arab/Muslim people and others. The third section is focused on working with Arab and Muslim clients and practical suggestions for "indirect" rather than direct approaches. Dwairy talks about the frustrations he experienced trying to apply the Western methods of his own training to his Arab/Muslim clients with their more collectivistic and authoritarian values that contrast with the more internalized and personal issues addressed by Western methods.

This book is not about indigenous Arab/Muslim alternative therapies but rather a bridge between Western and non-Western cultures, as Dwairy describes the task in the conclusion to his book: "A culturally sensitive approach in psychology is very important in this era of globalization, when Western culture is often offered as the ultimate choice for all peoples, regardless of their heritage or culture. Mental health professionals have much knowledge to share; their input can help develop greater understanding of and empathy for the cultures of others and promote pluralism within globalization." His focus is on shared characteristics and against simplistic stereotypes. Sometimes Western methods treat the abstract test profile as more real than the actual client.

This book provides not only a journey, an adventure, a metaphor to life itself, and a series of stories to help the reader understand the Arab/Muslim client, but also a better understanding of how clients from that cultural context are likely to perceive the Western counselor. There is an urgent need to reframe the counseling process in a global context. Without that larger and more inclusive perspective counseling is in danger of becoming the tool of a majority culture elite defined by a tendency to impose, without justification, a narrowly defined monocultural perspective favorable to the social/economic/political/military special interest group sometimes labeled as "Western."

Paul B. Pedersen

Preface

The reader of this book will find within it ideas and models based on my 25 years of experience in clinical, educational, developmental, and medical psychology among Arabs, Muslims, Jews, and Americans, but mainly among Palestinian Arabs. I studied for my master's degree in clinical psychology at Haifa University in Israel, during which time I received some practical training at Jewish psychological centers in Israel. Thus both my theoretical study and practical training were based on the Western-oriented theories of psychology. Immediately after graduation I opened the first psychological center in my native city, Nazareth, which is the largest Palestinian Arab city in Israel.

The main experience I remember from my first year of work in Nazareth is that my clients seemed to be different from those described in the context of psychological theories. They reacted differently to my diagnostic and therapeutic interventions. They tended to focus on their external circumstances and were unable to address internal and personal issues. Terms such as self, self-actualization, ego, and personal feelings were alien to them. They emphasized duty, the expectations of others, the approval of others, and family issues. In conversation with my clients, the task of distinguishing between the client's personal needs, opinions, or attitudes and those of the family was almost impossible. This experience was very disappointing, even threatening, to a new and enthusiastic psychologist who believed that the psychology he had learned was universal and should therefore work as well among Palestinian Arabs as among any other people. Using the premise "If I did it, they can do it," during the first years in Nazareth I tried to fit the clients to the "Western-oriented psychology," using a variety of educational community projects to mold them. Only after several years did I realize that it was I who should be fitting my theories to the community. Since then I have been trying to adjust Western theories to fit our social and cultural reality.

My writings are therefore not of one whose orientation is solely Western and who looks at and judges the Arabic culture only from a Western perspective. Rather, they are based both on my personal experience with the Arabic culture in which I was raised and which I have studied for many years, and on my formal learning and professional training in Western psychology. I have tried to discover where Western approaches to psychology do or do not fit the Arab or

Muslim culture and how counselors may employ the Arab/Muslim values, customs, and norms in counseling and therapy. This book does not address traditional Arabic and Muslim healing practices that are common in these societies.

In this book I extend the scope and deepen and enrich some of the ideas presented in my previous book *Cross-Cultural Counseling: The Arab-Palestinian Case*, published in 1998. I extend the Palestinian case and present a more coherent conceptualization of the personality of all Arab/Muslims, as well as intervention therapy among them. In the first part of this book the history, demographics, and culture of Arabs and Muslims in the world and in the United States are introduced. In the second and third parts a culturally sensitive revision is made of the theories of development, personality, assessment, psychopathology, counseling, and psychotherapy. My spouse, Khawla Abu-Baker, who is a family therapist and an expert on Arab and Muslim women's issues, has contributed two chapters, sharing with the readers her valuable experience among Arab/Muslim families in the United States, Palestine, and Israel.

While this book highlights some basic psycho-cultural features of Arabs and Muslims, I urge readers to avoid two main biases that Hare-Mustin and Marecek (1988) discuss in respect to gender differences: alpha and beta biases. If I borrow these biases and apply them to cultural rather than gender differences, then alpha bias indicates the exaggeration of differences existing between cultures. The existence of psychocultural features in one culture does not exclude these features in some way or degree from another culture and does not deny many shared universal features. Cultural features are always relative and not absolute; therefore, if we claim that Arabs/Muslims live in a collective/authoritarian culture, this does not mean that no other nation shares the same culture in one way or another. On the other hand, beta bias involves a denial of the differences that do exist between cultures. This bias may be called "color blindness" toward cultures; its proponents claim that all people are the same. When we compare cultures, we need to remember that similarities should not make us blind to diversity, and vice versa. In addition, I suggest that readers also avoid a third bias, namely, generalization within the culture, which looks at cultures from a stereotypic perspective, denying individual differences and variations within the same culture.

The September 11 attacks have distorted the real image of Arab and Muslim cultures. Since then, Arab and Muslim citizens in the West have become victims of misunderstanding or accusations. I hope this book will enable the Western reader to know these people better and will contribute both to the development of cultural sensitivity among practitioners who work with Arabs and Muslims and to the world effort to develop cross-cultural psychology.

PART I

UNDERSTANDING THE
PSYCHOCULTURAL HERITAGE

Chapters 1, 2, and 3 introduce Arab/Muslim history and culture to Western practitioners. The main intent here is to describe the collective and authoritarian features of Arab/Muslim societal behavioral norms. Readers will notice that, for Arabs/Muslims, history is not only a matter of a past background and heritage but also a significant component of their daily experience in the present. Similarly, culture is also not only a collective matter but also an inseparable component of the individual's self.

The presence of history and culture in the lives of Arab/Muslim immigrants in the West is very noticeable. These components become distinct and influential when immigrants are exposed to a different culture. Practitioners who are aware of these components are better able to understand their clients and the contribution of the Arab/Muslim history and culture to their behavior, emotions, and attitudes. Chapter 3 gives a more precise description of the Arab/Muslim immigrant. Generally speaking, these immigrants lead their lives against two cultural backgrounds: the Arab/Muslim one that is described in this part of the book and the Western individualistic one. The amount of influence exerted by each culture may vary from one client to another, depending on the client's level of acculturation and assimilation into Western life. Simply put, some clients are more "Arab/Muslim" while others are more "Western." This book may help clinicians understand the Arab/Muslim portion of the client's personality.

Clinicians who work with Arab/Muslim immigrants may wonder whether the psychocultural characteristics described in this book refer more to Arabs/Muslims in the United States or to those in Arab/Muslim countries. Clinicians need first to evaluate the level of acculturation and decide the extent to which each client is "Arab/Muslim" or "Western." Based on this evaluation, clinicians can adjust their attitudes and interventions regardless of the client's residency.

Chapter 1

The Arab People and Islam Religion

Western counselors and therapists who work with Arab and/or Muslim clients usually realize immediately that they are not dealing with an independent individual, and discover the tremendous impact of the family, culture, and heritage on the client's thoughts, attitudes, feelings, and behavior. The first part of this book is therefore devoted to describing the cultural heritage with which these clients come to therapy.

Islam is considered the third and most recent of the world's great monotheistic religions, the other two being Judaism and Christianity, to which it is closely related. All three religions are products of the Semitic spiritual life. In contemporary terms, Semitism or anti-Semitism is associated with Jews; but, in fact, both Arabs and Jews are Semitic peoples.

A BRIEF HISTORY

Long before the appearance of Christianity and Islam, Arabs lived in Najd (Arabia) and the Syrian deserts. To survive the toughness of the desert, they lived in a tribal nomadic system, moving with their families, camels, sheep, and horses to places where oases and grass could be found. Because they lived in a geographic location that links Asia, Africa, and Europe, Arabs worked in trade and transportation of goods between the three continents. At this time Arabs were pagan (although later on some became Jewish or Christian). This pre-Islamic period is called the *Jahiliyah* (period of ignorance), because Arabic tribes were then excessive in their violence, tribal revenge and retaliations, hedonistic lifestyle, alcohol abuse, polygamy, and abusive attitude to women.

Islam had its beginnings in the early seventh century (AD 610) in Mecca, a town in the western Arabian Peninsula. The prophet Mohammad began to exhort men and women to reform themselves morally and to submit to the will of God, as expressed in revelations to him from God. These revelations were accepted as divine messages by Mohammad and his adherents and were later collected in a book, the Qur'an. Islam not only brought moral and social reform that put an end to the Jahiliyah, but it also united all the Arabic tribes into one Islamic nation. The religion prohibited alcohol, and laid down strict and clear social, economic, and political rules that ensured relative social equality and justice. Since Islam was revealed to the Arab prophet Mohammad in the biggest Arab tribe, Quraysh, in the biggest Arab city in Arabia, Mecca, and since its holy book, the Qur'an, was written in Arabic, the Arabic history and language became central to the Muslims' history and life. As the influence of Islam expanded so did the Arabic world.

After the pre-Islamic Jahiliyah, the history of Muslims and Arabs can be seen as divided into three main periods: Islamic state, stagnation period, and the new revival period.

Islamic State

Within one decade of its advent, Islam had spread from Arabia to Asia, Africa, and Europe, and was adopted by non-Arab people such as the Persians, Turks, Indians, Mongols, Balkans, and the Spanish. The glory of this Islamic state lasted from the seventh to the fourteenth century. During this period large cities and mosques were built, and the Arab lifestyle changed from that of nomads to that of peasants and town dwellers. The Arabic nation experienced its "renaissance" period while Europe was drowning in its medieval dark period: Islamic arts, architecture, and poetry flourished. The state employed scholars, philosophers, and wise men to document the knowledge that Arab and other cultures (Greek, Indian, Persian, and Egyptian) had developed. Arabs contributed greatly to human knowledge in the fields of philosophy, mathematics, medicine, astronomy, occult sciences, and sciences (Hourani, 1991); in fact, the first mental health hospitals in the world were built during this period in Baghdad, Cairo, and Damascus (Okasha, 1993).

Stagnation Period

The stagnation period started in the end of the fourteenth century and continued until the eighteenth century. During this period Arabs were ruled by other non-Arab Muslim nations such as the Mamluks and Ottomans, and the western part of the Islamic Empire (Andalusia) fell into European hands. Interestingly, the Arabic stagnation period coincided with the European renaissance period. During the period of the Islamic state, when Arabs were the rulers, the Arab identity was not distinct from the Islamic. During the stagnation period the Arabs became divided between loyalty to the Muslim non-Arab rulers in their fight against the European Crusaders and opposition to these rulers. For the first time in Arab history, however, the Arabic identity became distinct from the Islamic.

At the end of that period the pan-Arabic movement emerged, and Arabic and Islamic identities became distinct one from the other.

New Revival Period

In the nineteenth century the Arab and Muslim worlds were exposed to and influenced by European culture in a variety of ways. This was a period of revival during which Arabs and Muslims started to work on defining their identity in relation to the West. The cultural debate now focused on questions of traditionalism and authenticity versus modernity and Westernization, while national forces continued to struggle against the European rulers to achieve national independence. At the end of World War II, European rule in the Arabic world ended, creating a sectarian region divided into several independent Arab and Muslim states.

DEMOGRAPHIC PICTURE

Today Muslims number about 1.2 billion people worldwide. In addition to the Arabs, this number includes the populations of a variety of nations that have adopted Islam as their religion, such as Indonesia, Malaysia, Pakistan, Afghanistan, Iran, and Turkey. In all these countries the majority of the people practice Islam as their religion, but they have maintained their indigenous language and culture.

The Arabs today number about 285 million, living mainly in 22 Arab countries, such as Saudi Arabia, Morocco, and Egypt. A few million live elsewhere in the world as emigrants. The vast majority of Arabs are Muslims, but large Christian Arab minorities live in Egypt, Lebanon, Jordan, Syria, and Palestine, and elsewhere in the world. Christian Arabs are Arabs in all senses: they speak Arabic and share the same Arabic cultural heritage, norms, and values, but maintain and practice their Christian religion. Figure 1.1 shows that the majority of Arab people have adopted Islam as their religion, as well as Christianity. A wide variety of nations have adopted Islam as their religion, most of which are not Arab.

MUSLIMS AND ARABS IN THE INDIVIDUALISM-COLLECTIVISM DIMENSION

Individualism-collectivism and liberalism-authoritarianism are two major dimensions along which cultures across the world are spread and according to

Figure 1.1. The Arabs and Muslims

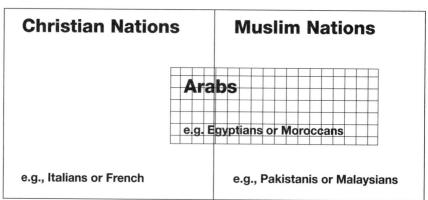

which they can be differentiated and identified (Dwairy, 1997c, 1998a; Fiske, 1990, 1992; Hofstede 1980, 1991; Triandis, 1995). Triandis (1995) defines *individualism* as "a social pattern that consists of loosely linked individuals who view themselves as independent of collectives; are primarily motivated by their own preferences, needs, rights, and contracts they have established with others; give priority to their personal goals over the goals of others; and emphasize rational analyses of the advantages and disadvantages to associating with others" and *collectivism* as "a social pattern consisting of closely linked individuals who see themselves as part of one or more collective (family, coworkers, tribe, nation); are primarily motivated by the norms of, and duties imposed by, those collectives; are willing to give priority to the goals of those collectives over their own personal goals; and emphasize their connectedness to members of their collectives" (p. 2). The liberalism-authoritarianism dimension parallels other dimensions referred to as "horizontal-vertical" or "looseness-tightness" (Triandis, 1990), or "weak versus strong uncertainty avoidance" or "small versus large power distance" (Hofstede 1980).

Collective and/or authoritarian cultures emphasize family integrity, harmony, interdependence, saving face, authority, and hierarchy within the collective. Family integrity, obedience, and conformity values override competition, pleasure, and self-fulfillment. Social and geographical mobility is limited. People in these cultures tend to live near their parents and their behavior is regulated by collective norms that are more important than the individual's attitudes. The *self* is defined as an appendage of the collective, and an individual's identity is associated with social affiliation to the family or tribe rather than to personal qualities or achievements; social relationships are close and cooperative and involve much hospitality (Triandis, 1990).

Historically, collectivism/authoritarianism characterized the preindustrial societies in the West. In the Middle Ages and the beginning of the Renaissance in Europe, individuals lived in a state of unity with their families or clans. Their rights were not recognized, and they spent their whole lives working, socializing, and marrying within the appropriate social class, with little chance of moving from one class to another. People served the interests of the ruler, while the state took no responsibility for the welfare of its citizens. The family or the clan was therefore the main institution that took care of the individual. (From here on, "collectivism" may stand for "collectivism/authoritarianism.")

In the eighteenth century, however, social, political, and economic development in the West, such as industrialization and the French Revolution, accelerated the process of democracy and liberalism leading to the establishment of national democratic states. Once the state took responsibility for the welfare of its citizens, they were no longer dependent on their families for survival. They worked in industry, companies, or state institutions and bought the goods that the family had previously provided. Within this climate, the individual-family interdependence faded and individualism emerged (Dwairy, 1998a; Fromm, 1941, 1976).

Countries characterized by "individualism" imbue their citizens with the belief that the right to vote means that they share in the process of political decision making and in determining the destiny of society. However, within this system much of the power that influences peoples' lives is actually invisible. The political system shares the ruling of the state with large companies and corporations, which are capable of exerting control over the political system as well as education, culture, and the media. Political campaigns are financed by donations from large companies. The independence of the media, education, art, and sports is far from a reality. Individualism/liberalism has, in fact, substituted the interdependence between an individual and the family or tribe with a new interdependence with the state. (From here on, "individualism" may stand for "individualism/liberalism.")

In the Arab and Islamic world, however, the social, political, and economic changes that took place in the West did not occur, and thus the Arab and Islamic states did not take over the responsibility for providing all of their citizens' needs. In these countries people retained the interdependent relationship with their families, and the family is still responsible for raising and educating the children, finding jobs and housing for young adults, and providing protection and economic help in critical times. In addition, because of the vital interdependence between the individual and the family, familial authority still plays the role that the courts and law enforcement agencies play in western states. The family is authorized to judge the individual's behavior and punish any deviation that is conceived as threatening the family interests or harmony. Unlike in Western countries, where law courts and the police force are the entities that impose punishments, in societies where individual-family interdependence prevails, it is the family that assumes this responsibility; therefore, psychological and physical punishments are still commonly used by the family to discipline and socialize its children.

As people become affluent, they become financially self-sufficient and also socially and psychologically independent of their families or in-group (Triandis, 1990). Since most Arabs and Muslims are poor compared to Western citizens, they cannot renounce their interdependent relationship with their family or tribe, and therefore collectivism has a negative correlation with the gross national product (GNP) per capita (Hofstede, 1980). Table 1.1 presents indexes that denote the development level in seven Muslim, seven Arab countries, and four Western countries. Each group of Muslim and Arab countries includes the two most developed (H) and the two least developed (L) countries, along with three countries that fall in between the developmental extremes. While the gross domestic product (GDP) per capita in the Western countries is above $20,000, the GDP of the vast majority of the Muslim and Arab countries, is less than $10,000 per capita. Actually, the GDP of only a few Arab and Muslim countries even comes close to $10,000, most falling between $1,000 and $5,000 per capita. The range of development within the Muslim countries seems similar to that within the Arab countries. In many Arab and Muslim countries about a third of the population lives below the poverty line and 10–30% of adults are unemployed. In these countries the state does not provide necessary educational and health services, and therefore illiteracy and infant mortality rates are very high while life expectancy is significantly lower than that in the West. Of course, economics does not explain all of the variation in the collectivism dimension among different countries; cultural heritage counts too. Experts rate Malaysia (Muslim, not Arab) and Japan (neither Muslim nor Arab), two rich countries, as collective cultures (Levine, Norenzayan, & Philbrick, 2001). In fact, according to Hofstede's (1986) research, the culture of Malaysia, the richest Muslim country, is not only very much collective but also the most authoritarian of all the Muslim and Arab countries.

COMPATIBILITY AND DEVIATION IN THE ARAB AND MUSLIM WORLDS

The Arab and the Muslim worlds share the ethos of tribal collectivism and Islam, but are also influenced by their exposure to Western culture. The social system in both the Arab and the Muslim worlds tends to be authoritarian; the individual is very submissive to cultural and Islamic rules, which allow him limited scope for private choices. The centrality of the family or tribe and male dominance are common features in the two worlds. Despite some progress in

Table 1.1. Indexes of development in seven Muslim, seven Arab, and four Western countries.

	GDP (per capita)	Population (millions)	Below Poverty (percentage)	Unemployment (percentage)	Literacy (percentage)	Life expectancy (years)	Infant mortality (per 1000)
Muslim Countries							
Malaysia (H)	$9,000	23	8	4	NA	69	19
Iran (H)	$7,000	67	53	14	80	71	28
Turkey	$6,800	67	NA	11	85	71	46
Indonesia	$3,320	225	27	8	70	69	39
Pakistan	$2,100	148	35	6	NA	62	79
Bangladesh (L)	$1,750	134	36	35	NA	61	68
Afghanistan (L)	$800	28	NA	NA	36	47	145
Arab Countries							
Kuwait (H)	$15,100	2	NA	2	82*	76	11
Saudi Arabia (H)	$10,600	24	NA	NA	76*	68	49
Lebanon	$5,200	4	28	18	85*	69	27
Egypt	$3,700	71	23	12	55*	64	59
Syria	$3,200	17	15–25	20	73*	69	34
Sudan (L)	$1,360	37	NA	19	57*	57	85*
Somalia (L)	$550	8	NA	NA	NA	45	122
Western Countries							
USA	$36,300	281	13	5	97	77	7
Germany	$26,600	83	NA	9	NA	78	5
France	$25,700	60	NA	9	NA	79	4
UK	$25,300	60	17	5	NA	78	5

Based on Central Intelligence Agency Web, November 2003 (www.reference-guides.com/cia_world_factbook).
* Based on *Arab Human Development Report* by the United Nations Development Programme, 2002.
H = Most developed
L = least developed

the last few decades, democratic values and political rights remain limited, and the citizens of most Arab and Muslim states still rely for their survival on the family or tribe rather than on the state (United Nations Development Programme [UNDP], 2002).

Despite these similar cultural features, significant differences and local influences can also be noticed among the countries within each world. Nevertheless, the variation within the Arab world is similar to that within the Muslim one. These variations seem minor when compared to the deviation of both worlds from the Western individualistic world. Indeed, based on survey data of the values of people in more than 50 countries around the world, the Arabs of Egypt, Lebanon, Libya, Kuwait, Iraq, Saudi Arabia, and United Arab Emirates, as well as the Muslims of Indonesia, Iran, Malaysia, and Pakistan, scored high in collectivism and authoritarianism. Indonesia, the most populated Muslim country, ranked 47th out of the 53 countries and regions assessed, whereas Britain ranked 3rd on this dimension (Hofstede, 1980, 1986). These differences in the collectivism dimension are related to the social interaction between individuals in these societies. Indonesian respondents, for instance, were more willing to offer support to others than were their British counterparts (Goodwin & Giles, 2004).

The Arab Human Development Report 2002, released by the United Nations (UNDP, 2002), provides important demographic information concerning the development of 285 million Arabs in 22 countries. Because of its high fertility rate, children and juveniles between 0 and 18 years of age make up about 50% of the Arab population. The percentage of urbanization varies widely, ranging from 23% in Yemen and 24% in Somalia to 91% in Qatar and 96% in Kuwait. The rate of unemployment reaches about 20% or more in Algeria, Morocco, and Oman and 55% among Palestinians in the occupied territories.

The Arab countries have the highest level of extreme poverty in the world. One out of five people lives on less than $2 per day. It is true that some Arab countries are wealthy, such as Saudi Arabia, Kuwait, Qatar, United Arab Emirates, and Bahrain, but the combined population of these countries amounts to about 8% of the Arab world population. The oil that was discovered in these countries in the middle of the twentieth century is the main source of their wealth. Of the countries considered to be developing or poor, among the most impoverished are Djibouti, Mauritania, Oman, Somalia, and Sudan. A similar division exists among Muslim countries. Some are considered economically developed, such as Iran, Turkey, Indonesia, and Malaysia; while others, such as Pakistan and Afghanistan, are poor.

Poor economic conditions influence the health and education of both Arab and Muslim societies. Life expectancy varies from about 45 years in poor Arab (e.g., Somalia) and Muslim countries (e.g., Afghanistan) to 69 years and over in rich Arab (e.g., Kuwait and United Arab Emirates) and Muslim countries (e.g., Malaysia and Iran). The infant mortality rate in the poor Arab and Muslim countries reaches 99 infants per thousand in Yemen, 85 in Sudan, and 145 in Afghanistan. While the adult literacy rate of the world population is about 79%, the rate is about 60% in the Arab world. Two-thirds of illiterate Arabs are women.

It is important to mention here that generalization is an inherent cost paid in any study concerning cultural features of a nation: One can always say that a given feature does not fit all the people in one specific national group or that it fits another national group as well. Having said that, I can state that collectivism and authoritarianism are two prevailing cultural features that differentiate the Arab and Muslim worlds from the West, even though many countries within both worlds have been influenced by specific local factors. For instance, within the Muslim world Indonesia and Malaysia have been influenced by East Asian culture, Pakistan by Indian, and Turkey by European, but none of these influences can be generalized to the whole Muslim world. Similarly, within the Arab world one may identify Franco phonic as well as African influences in some North African Arab countries, and Anglo phonic and Turkish influences in some of the eastern Arab countries. Beyond these local influences, I did not find in the literature any common exclusive cultural feature in the Muslim world that does not also apply to the Arab world, and vice versa. Therefore the prototypic culture of the two worlds is very compatible.

SUMMARY

Arabs and Muslims have a similar collective experience and heritage. They both share the Islamic collective/authoritarian heritage, the centrality of the Arabic ethos and language, and the history of oppression by the Western occupier. Their social, political, and economic system today is similar. The majority of Arabs and Muslims are poor and lack access to basic state services, and they therefore continue to rely for their survival on their familial or tribal system. In both Muslim and Arabic societies, collectivism and authoritarianism are prevalent. People's lives are conducted according to family or tribal norms, values, will, and goals. The cultural differences between Arab and Muslim countries are mainly quantitative and are minor compared to the differences between the Arab and Muslim worlds, on one hand, and the Western world, on the other.

Chapter 2

The Arab/Muslim Culture

The collective values, thinking system, style of life, customs, and norms constitute the culture of any group of people. In order to understand a culture, one must first understand the collective experience of that group. The main factors in the collective experience of Arabs and many other Muslims that have shaped their culture are the tribal Bedouin experience in the desert, the rise of Islam, and exposure to the West.

COLLECTIVE TRIBAL BEDOUIN LIFE

Because Islam first appeared in Arabia and then spread to other areas, both the Arabic and Islamic cultures were influenced by life in the desert (Abd al-Karim, 1990). Before Islam, Arabs and non-Arabs in the Arabian, Syrian, North African, Iranian, and Afghani deserts lived in a nomadic tribal system that enabled them to survive in tough natural conditions. To maintain this system, a strict patriarchal hierarchical authority was needed to protect the collective interests of the tribe. Life within a tribal system is characterized by the fanatic identification of its members with the tribe (*'asabiya*), and full submission and obedience to the tribal leadership. The behavior of a member within a tribal system is directed by tribal norms rather than by that individual's own ideas or decisions. Tribe members are expected to act always to maintain the group's cohesion and to avoid any action that might weaken it. Mutual support within the tribe and a collective stand against external invaders or threats are basic attitudes in tribal life (Hourani, 1991).

After the advent of Islam in the seventh century, all Muslims, both Arab and non-Arab, were united within one state. The Islamic state did not weaken the tribal system, but rather was built on it, becoming like a confederation of tribes (Al-Jabiri, 1991b). A more modern version of this tribal system is still found in all Arab and many other Muslim states today; many of the Arab states are actually ruled by tribes or large families. Attempts in the Arab world to develop a democratic government have led to the absorption of the tribe and other sect affiliations within the political system (Dwairy, 1998a). The distribution of votes in political elections is dominated strongly by the familial, clan, tribal, religious, or sect affiliation of the Arab and Muslim voters (Al-Haj, 1989; Ghanem, 2001). Before elections to the local councils in Arab villages in Israel, one can find headlines in Arabic newspapers such as: "Nominating Hassan Athamni as the family candidate in the local council elections," "Abdelhai family promotes their candidate, Ma'amoon Abdelhai," or "A'azem family presents two candidates." (*Panorama* [Taibi, Israel], August 29, 2003, pp. 25, 31, 37).

The tribal system does not acknowledge the individualist, who is abhorred and considered a disturber of the collective harmony. In Islam too, the idea of the individual in the philosophical meaning of the world and nature is nonexistent. Traditional societies produced Muslims who were submissive to the group will. Individuality in such a system is discouraged, and its development is brought to a halt at the point where it may threaten the authority of the leader. A mere shadow of an individual who has no autonomy is thus created (Umlil, 1985). Many contemporary Arab and Muslim scholars claim that tribalism still prevails and influences social and political domains in Arab/Muslim societies today (Abu-Baker, 1998; Al-Jabiri, 1991a, 2002; Barakat, 2000).

Collectivism survives today, not solely as a result of the continuation of the ancestral tribal heritage, but also for prevailing sociopolitical and economic reasons. Unlike modern Western societies, where the state has taken over the responsibility for its citizens' survival, most modern Arab/Muslim states do not assume this responsibility. The tribe, therefore, or the extended family or clan, still performs this function. In rural areas of Arab/Muslim countries, their citizens are often deprived of basic governmental services. In Saudi Arabia, one of the richest Arab and Muslim countries for example, the state still has no official registration of all its citizens. Many Saudis are simply ignored by the government. A similar situation is found in Afghanistan, Turkey, Iran, Sudan, and many other Arab/Muslim countries. In these countries young couples rely on their collective tribe or family rather than on the state for child care and education, labor, housing, and protection. This interconnectedness among members of a collective tribe is reflected also in the culture and structure of individual families. Fisek and Kagitcibasi (1999) claim that, despite industrialization, urbanization, and increased educational opportunity, the Turkish culture is still closer to the collective and authoritarian pole, and the prototypic Turkish family is characterized by a strong hierarchy and a high degree of proximity, closeness, and interconnectedness. The authoritarianism in the Turkish family that they observe is manifested in a "gender and generational hierarchy" (p. 80), according to which women and the young are dominated by men and older members of the family. This hierarchical structure is characteristic also of the larger sociocultural system among Arabs and Muslims; males and elders have a higher status than females and young people.

Collectivism among Arabs/Muslims indicates affiliation to groups that hold an intermediate position between the individual and the nation, such as the tribe, the extended family, clan (*hamula*), or the family. This affiliation may contradict the individual's needs on the one hand (such as when the family opposes a romantic relationship), or the national or universal affiliation on the other (such as when a family member considers voting for a national party versus a party that has made a deal with the family). When this kind of contradiction exists, the collective interests prevail over the individual and the nation (Barakat, 2000). Furthermore, in the absence of state institutions and services, loyalty and adherence to the collective is very practical for the purpose of survival, while independence and departure from the tribal system is almost impossible and is counterproductive for its members. Most of the Arab/Muslim economies are therefore based on the family unit rather than on the company unit (Barakat, 2000).

Diversity Within the Collective/Authoritarian Arab/Muslim Societies

As mentioned before, Arab and Muslim countries were influenced by local history and culture in Southeast Asia, North Africa, and the Middle East. These local influences have affected how the different countries are distributed along the continuum between the poles of authoritarian/collective and liberal/individualistic societal models. For instance Malaysia, Pakistan, Saudi Arabia, and Libya are more authoritarian and collective than Lebanon, Turkey, Tunis, and Egypt. Communities inhabiting urban areas are less authoritarian and less collective than those in rural areas. Among some social layers of urban society, educated middle- and upper-class people can be found who have adopted a moderate collectivist culture or even one that is close to being individualistic. Arabs/Muslims who learn or work in the West and those who have immigrated to the West tend to adopt a more moderate collectivist culture. Initially, assimilation of immigrants takes place in the economic, entertainment, and political arenas, and later may embrace family life and the socialization of the children (see Chapter 3).

The diversity within the Arab/Muslim world is increasing with time. A rapid process of urbanization is taking place, which is increasing the disparity between rural neglected and urban developed areas (Zakariya, 1999). Certain areas, such as the Persian Gulf countries, have been passing through an unusually rapid transition since the discovery of oil in the first half of the twentieth century. The oil countries, previously characterized by poor traditional tribal life, became rich countries able to acquire the most developed Western facilities and technology and build new modern cities for their citizens to inhabit. Because of the need for experts and trained labor, many of the inhabitants of these countries are now foreign. A rapid process of transition and acculturation is therefore taking place in these countries. The effects of industrialization, urbanization, and increased educational opportunity have not affected all sectors of the Arab or Muslim societies equally: "While some sectors like the urban elite are seemingly indistinguishable from the prototypic Western type, other sectors remain unchanged, and some even seem to be choosing to return to an even more traditional lifestyle" (Fisek & Kagitcibasi, 1999, p. 81).

Despite the modernization and urbanization that have taken place in the Arab world in the last century, tribal Bedouin values are still in effect and dominant in many contemporary Arab societies. Values such as the hospitality and generosity that were vital in the desert, where modern transportation, hotels, and restaurants were nonexistent, continue to direct people's social behavior in modern cities. Good social relationships with Arab people typically necessitate visiting their homes and sharing meals with their families. In its tribal Bedouin meaning, honor is another value that was very practical in desert life and it continues to be an important value today. Honorable behavior is that which maintains the group cohesion and serves its interests, while shameful behavior is that which tends to disrupt or impair that cohesion (Patai, 1983). For some traditional Arab societies today, honor is still such a valuable collective asset that, if a member stains it, the whole family or clan stands as one to punish the perpetrator.

The Collective Culture in Counseling

Counselors who work with clients having an Arab/Muslim or any other collective cultural background are encouraged to give special attention to understanding the relationships within the family (conflicts, coalitions, and force balances) and the status of the client in the family. Counselors who deny the family and instead focus on personal issues may miss the point and make the client, who is totally enmeshed in the family, feel misunderstood. Therefore, assessment of the level of authoritarianism/collectivism of the client and the family is one of the first tasks of the counselor. Judgmental attitudes toward the submission of the client to the familial authority should be avoided. Counselors are encouraged to try to understand the rationale of this submission from within and to help the client find support and better coalitions within the family (see Chapters 6, 9, and 10).

VALUES AND TEACHINGS OF ISLAM

Muslim and non-Muslim Arabic culture is deeply influenced by the heritage and history of Islam, from its beginning in the seventh century to the revival period in the nineteenth and twentieth centuries (see Chapter 1).

The Qur'an, the book of divine revelations to Mohammad, and the Sunna, the body of Islamic practice based on the sayings (Hadith) and deeds of the prophet Mohammad, became the basic references for Islamic life. Because the language of the Qur'an is a rhetorical and metaphorical Arabic language, the interpretation (tafsir) of its verses and of the Hadith was open to debate. As a result, different Islamic scholars ('ulama) and groups have adopted different Islamic beliefs, attitudes, and styles of life. Among the many sects that have emerged within Islam, the two largest are: the Sunnis and Shiites. Sunnis tend to adhere literally to the teachings of Qur'an and Sunna on how one should lead one's life on earth, while the Shiites (among them Sufis) tend to be more spiritualistic, using prayer to come closer to the divine reality of God. The history of Islam is much more than just a history. The prophet Mohammad, Islamic historical figures, and Islamic teachings are very much alive in the minds and hearts of many Muslims today and affect their daily behavior. Tens of Arabic satellites broadcast these teachings and directives many hours a day to Muslims throughout the world. Terms such as Sunna, Hadith, 'ulama, and tafsir are part of the daily jargon of many Arabs and Muslims.

In addition to the varying approaches to Islam of these and other sects, Muslims are also differentiated by their degree of "fundamentalism." Among Islamic societies today one can find extreme fundamentalist leaders and groups who espouse complete rejection of Western culture and justify the social repression and oppression of women in the name of Islam. At the other extreme are the Islamic scholars who emphasize the democratic values, conciliation, and social justice of Islam. In fact, the majority of societies adopt a moderate and open version of Islam. However, the fundamentalist Islamic groups including the violent and terroristic Bin Laden and the Taliban in Afghanistan are at best more vociferous and receive wide coverage in the media, which gives Western societies the wrong impression about Islam as a whole and leads them to feel threatened by all Arabs and Muslims.

The Five Pillars of Islam

The five fundamental tenets of Islam that are shared by all Islamic groups are:

1. *Shahada*: the profession of faith ("There is no God but Allah, and Mohammad is His Prophet.")
2. *Siyam*: fasting in the holy month of Ramadan.
3. *Salah*: praying five times a day.
4. *Zakah*: a tax that is devoted to providing financial help to the poor.
5. *Haj*: the pilgrimage to Mecca.

These tenets order Muslims to submit and pray to one God (*shahada, salah,* and *haj*), learn to control their instincts (*siyam*), and be empathic to the poor and offer them help (*zakah*). A true Islamic fundamentalist should adhere to and fulfill these five fundamental tenets. Antagonism and hostility to the West is far divorced from any true Islamic fundamental belief. On the contrary, Islam is very clear about the need to accept and respect other monotheistic religions, such as Christianity and Judaism. There are many verses in the Qur'an and in the Hadith that preach the advantages of diversity and the value of tolerance between nations. Extreme fundamentalist Muslim groups employ different inter-pretations of Islam (other than Qur'an or Sunna) to inflame antagonism against the West, an antagonism which had its roots in Western imperialism and uncon-ditional support of the Israeli occupation, rather than in religious differences.

Islam provides strict rules and laws (*Shari'ah*), based on Qur'an and Sunna, according to which the personal, familial, social, economic, and political life must be led. Islam not only involves faith and prayer to God, but also legislates almost every issue in life. Islam is a social religion that suggests a balanced order in society. It orders Muslims to balance their worship of God with their enjoyment of life on earth. *"Wabtag'i fema a'tak Allah al-dar el-aakhera wala tansa nasibak men al-dunia"* (Al-Qusas #77). [But seek, by means of that which God has given you, to attain the abode of the hereafter and do not forget your share in this world.] Basic to the teachings of Islam is finding legal ways to satisfy human instincts and needs. Unlike Christianity, which tends to ignore or deny human sexuality, Islam specifically deals with sexual issues and suggests legal ways of sexual control of women (e.g., veiling) and provides sexual vents for men (e.g., polygamy). Most Islamic scholars consider these legislations to be progressive reforms, compared to the situation in Jahiliyah, when some tribes used to kill female newborns (*w'ad el-banat*), but legislations about gender is-sues have provoked much debate in Islamic societies. Fortunately, among Mus-lim countries today only Saudi Arabia enforces the veiling of women, and in many Muslim countries, such as Tunisia and Turkey, state laws prohibit veiling and polygamy.

Fatima Mernissi (1992; 1993), a feminist sociologist, appeals for a differen-tiation to be made between the Qur'an and Sunna, which include the fundamen-tals of Islam, and any further interpretations (tafsir) that were made by the schol-ars (*'ulama*) during the last 14 centuries. She claims that the later interpretations were influenced by politics and the interests of the *'ulama,* and that therefore they are contradictory and open to debate.

Islam emphasizes the role of reason and education in people's lives (Al-Jabiri, 1991b). The first order that Mohammad received from God was to recite. He asked, "What shall I recite?" and then he heard the angel's voice ordering him: "Recite: in the name of thy Lord who created, created man of a blood-clot. Recite: and thy Lord is the most bountiful, who taught by the pen, taught man what he knew not." The Qur'an is full of verses that ask Muslims to reason (*'aql*) and to think. Unlike the Western construction of thinking, however, the

Islamic meaning of thinking and reason is related to morals rather than to intelligence or creativity. A wise person is one who knows the teaching of Islam and how to deduce answers for a current problem from the Qur'an, the Prophet's teachings, and the *'ulama* heritage (Al-Jabiri, 2002).

Islam suggests two ways of thinking. One is the major way of thinking among the Sunni branch of Islam which is called *qeyas* (or knowing through mensuration or measurement). The other is adopted by the Shiite branch and is called *'irfan* (or knowing through enlightenment during prayer) (Al-Jabiri, 1991a). In *qeyas*, the Muslim must measure a new problem or situation by a former similar one that had been addressed or answered by the Qur'an or Sunna and then apply the old answer or solution to the new problem and behave accordingly. As can be seen, the *qeyas* leaves no room for personal judgment, choice, or creative thinking. Therefore, the major function of the mind according to *qeyas* is to know how to understand analogies and how to follow directives. As for *'irfan*, the way to reach and understand the true reality is to overlook the material objective reality and look for directives through prayer and meditation to understand the divine reality. Neither *qeyas* nor *'irfan* show Muslims how to cope efficiently with the new challenges of the changing modern life (Dwairy, 1997c).

The Arab/Muslim mind tends to be past-oriented (*salafiya*), influenced by Islamic teachings that direct Muslims to look for answers through *qeyas* in the Islamic heritage. Therefore Arab/Muslim people tend to find refuge in their successful and prosperous past, hoping to find there salvation and a remedy for the defeat and helplessness they feel when faced with the flourishing West. Unfortunately, relying on the past to find answers to present and future problems has become counterproductive in the Arab/Muslim culture and mind. Instead of using the past collective experience to understand the present and to determine an updated plan for the future, many relate only to the past, intending to revive it in its former shape, and so deny the new developing reality (Al-Jabiri, 2002).

In addition to the past, Arabs/Muslims give authoritative value to language. Articulate language (*bayan*) may convince the listener more by its elegant wording than by the actual content of the argument expressed. Some attribute the effect of Qur'an to its highly articulate language (Al-Jabiri, 1991b). When past teachings are presented in an articulate language (a combination of *salafiya, qeyas,* and *bayan*), such as in a beautifully worded verse of Qur'an or Hadith, they become convincing and capable of overriding logic. This may explain the central role of proverbs in directing the lives of Arabs/Muslims, since proverbs are considered to summarize the wisdom of past experience in an articulate form.

Utilization of Islamic Ideas in Counseling

Counselors and psychotherapists who work with Muslim clients should bear in mind that Islam prohibits renunciation of the Islamic faith. They should therefore avoid any confrontation with Islam and try to help their clients find new answers and ways to change within Islamic teachings. Fortunately, as a result of the long history of Islamic debate, one can find within this heritage many Qur'an verses, Hadith directives, and proverbs that can be employed to facilitate therapeutic change.

Based on the fact that *qeyas* is the basic epistemological mechanism that Islam recommends to people in order to find their way in life, and in accordance with the fact that Arabs/Muslims frequently use inherited idioms and proverbs in their daily discourse, counselors and therapists may employ this cognitive mechanism in therapy. Metaphor therapy (see Chapter 11) is perhaps the best suited to *qeyas* because in metaphor therapy the client actually gains insight into his or her problem by virtue of understanding the metaphor being discussed; it is consistent with the *qeyas* that directs the Muslim to solve the current problem through understanding a similar past event that the Qur'an or Sunna has already discussed.

One major idea that may be employed to make a strictly adherent client rethink his or her attitudes is the centrality of ʿ*aql* (reason) in Islam. Thus the therapist may remind a client of the Islamic teaching to use ʿ*aql*. In psychological terms, "activating the ʿ*aql*" means activating the client's ego to find compromises and realistic answers. Knowing that the *qeyas* is the basic epistemological way to truth for the orthodox Muslim, the therapist may employ some Qur'anic verses, Hadith, and proverbs that suggest a new and different attitude to the problem in order to help the client revise and rethink his or her attitude.

When clients attribute their attitudes to Islam, therapists may direct them to differentiate between the five fundamental tenets of Islam, the Qur'an, or Sunna, on the one hand and the interpretations of the scholars that some may say justify their attitude, on the other. The interpretations of the ʿ*ulama* are actually so full of contradictory references that one can find there almost any attitude one wants. Clients may therefore be directed to look for alternative Islamic interpretations that may help them revise their attitudes and enable change.

There are many kinds of problems that can benefit from therapeutic use of Islamic teachings. I present here some examples concerning women's rights, stress and loss, and school violence.

Women's Rights. A discussion of attitudes toward women occasionally arises in therapy, and oppressive attitudes toward women are often attributed to Islam. Mernissi (1992; 1993) argues that most of the oppressive attitudes toward women are found in the interpretations (*tafsir*) of male scholars (ʿ*ulama*) and have nothing to do with true Islam. In her book *The Veil and the Male Elite: A Feminist Interpretation of Women's Rights in Islam*, she offers alternate open, flexible, and egalitarian Islamic interpretations that may be helpful when these issues arise in therapy. For example, parents who forbid their daughter to study at a university because they believe that Islam prohibits girls from learning may be reminded by the therapist of the first verse in Qur'an, directing the faithful to read (*iqra*' means recite*)*. In another example, a chauvinistic, controlling man or a submissive woman may both be reminded of the central role that the Prophet's wife 'Aisha played in matters of religion, politics, and the military. Additional examples of women's rights supplied by Islamic teachings are found in Mernissi's book.

Stress and Loss. Predestination is one core belief in Islam. The destiny of a person, for good or bad, is determined (*maktub)* by God, and nothing that God has not determined in advance will happen to anybody. This belief is documented in the verse, *"Qol lan yosibuna illa ma katab Allah lana howa mawlana wa'ala Allah falyatawakal el-mo'amenin"* (Al-tawbah #51). [Say: Nothing will befall us except what God has ordained. He is our Guardian. In God let the faithful put their trust.] The belief in predestination has been found to help clients accept, endure, and cope with stress, threat, and loss. Focusing on God's good intentions, therapists may encourage a client to endure stress, remain optimistic, and avoid hopelessness, by employing the verse, *"Fa'asa an takrahou shaia'an wayaja'alu Allah menhu khayran kathera"* (Al-nisaa #19). [It may well be that you dislike a thing which God has meant for your own abundant good.]

Counselors and therapists who deal with reactions to death may employ the religious beliefs of their clients to help them reframe the death and give it a meaning that helps them cope with the loss. Islam teaches that when a person dies during a national or religious struggle he will live eternally in heaven. This belief is documented in the verse, *"Wala tahsabanna alatheena qotilou fi sabeel Allah amwatan bal ahya'a 'and Rabbihem yorzaqoon"* (Al-A'mran #169). [Do not consider those who died for God dead but rather as living in God's place.] The notion of living beside God may explain how Palestinian mothers, who consider their sons martyrs, exhibit a satisfied reaction when their sons die as a result of an Israeli attack or as suicide bombers inside Israel. Another belief that has proved useful in the therapy of bereaved families is the belief in the reincarnation of souls, supported by the Shiite and Druze sects.

Clearly, the Islamic ideas that can be employed in therapy are too numerous to be included in this chapter, and Western therapists are not expected to be experts in Islam. They can, however, remind Muslim clients that beyond the five fundamental tenets Islamic heritage has diverse attitudes, and encourage clients to look for new answers to the issue under discussion by asking a religious leader or by reading Islamic sources. Clients may be referred to the interpretations of some well-known reformist Islamic scholars from the nineteenth and the twentieth centuries such as Al Tabari, Mohamad Abdu, Al-Afghani, and Al-Tahtawi, who, offered moderate, democratic, and egalitarian Islamic attitudes (see Hourani, 1983). This search for new meanings may have a therapeutic effect per se (Frankl, 1959).

School Violence. Islamic teachings may be employed to cope with school violence, as shown in the following example. During a teachers' meeting at which interventions for dealing with violence at school were being discussed, one religious Muslim teacher became annoyed and expressed his rejection of all the ideas related to trying to understand or accept the views of the students. He cited several Islamic interpretations that call for strict adherence to discipline and opposed our projects that seemed to him to be permissive. At the end of the meeting I approached him and expressed my respect for Islamic teachings and asked him to help me find verses or sayings from Qur'an or Hadith that direct people toward conciliation and forgiveness and condemn violence and aggression. In the next teachers' meeting he presented the material he had collected and was ready to serve as a staff head, working to spread Islamic ideas of conciliation and forgiveness among students and parents as a part of the school project against violence.

EXPOSURE TO WESTERN CULTURE

In the past, Arabs/Muslims saw Westerners as occupiers and oppressors in Africa and Asia. Today they see them as supporters or condoners of the Israeli occupation of Palestinian land. Nevertheless, they are fascinated by Western technology and science. They consume Western products and their scholars absorb Western theories and research findings. In the last few decades, especially after the fall of the Soviet Union, Arab/Muslim societies have been aggressively pushed by Western countries to adopt democratic and liberal political systems in their countries. These attempts are seen as threats to the collective aspect of the Arab/Muslim societies, and as hypocritical policies, because the human rights and liberty of people in these societies are abused by the West in the name of democracy, human rights, and, recently, the fight against terrorism.

For centuries Western imperialism suppressed all national movements that struggled for a national independence. Such movements would have precluded social development from tribal or familial interdependence to national state-citizen interdependence. Thus tribalism continued to prevail in Arab/Muslim societies, at least partly, by virtue of this policy of the West. The long exposure to the Western occupiers left its impact on the Arab/Muslim culture. Their imperialism fostered submission and helplessness among the people. Conversely, the exposure to a superior oppressor gave rise to inferiority feelings and brought about a process of identification with that oppressor. Therefore, the attitude toward the West is mixed with rage and antagonism, on the one hand, and identification and glorification, on the other.

No doubt the exposure to Westerners through imperialism or through the media, sciences, and technology has brought new individualistic values that challenge the Arab/Muslim collective traditions. From the nineteenth century until now the correct attitude toward Western culture has been profoundly debated in the Arab/Muslim world. Three main currents in this debate can be identified:

1. Fundamentalist: Calls for the restoration and revival of orthodox Arab/ Islamic values and lifestyles in an attempt to restore the glorious past.
2. Coordinating: Calls for openness, compromise, and reciprocal fertilization of ideas between the Arab/Muslim and Western cultures. Among the proponents of this are many Islamic scholars who appeared in the nineteenth and twentieth centuries, such as Al-Tahtawi, Al-Afghani, and Abdu.
3. Assimilating: Calls for abandoning old traditions and adopting the Western individualistic and liberal way (Hourani, 1983; Zakariya, 1999). Proponents of this view identify almost completely with the West and attribute the defeat and stagnation of the Arab/Muslim state to the Arab/ Islamic traditions.

In this debate the moderate stream is prevalent; nevertheless the fundamentalist stream is more vociferous and captures the attention of Western media.

Implications for Counseling

The Arab/Muslim collective experience vis-a-vis the West may be manifested explicitly or implicitly in counseling with a Western counselor. It may be displayed in transference and countertransference processes. As collectivists, many Arab/Muslim clients may bring their Arab/Muslim culture to the counseling session and consider the Western counselor as a representative of all that the West means for the Arab/Muslim. The Arab/Muslim client may express submissiveness to the counselor not only as transference of the child-parent relationship but also as transference of the Arab/Muslim–West relationship. Expressions of anger and rage, on the one hand, and inferiority feelings, shame, or fear of punishment, on the other, are expected components of an Arab/Muslim's transference toward a Western counselor. For some Arab or Muslim clients, an American therapist, for example, may represent the whole American regime and its policies toward the Arabic and Islamic nations. The transference may be expressed in terms of "we" (the Arabs) and "you" (the Americans). Therapists should not take any accusation of Americans personally, but rather help the client differentiate between the therapist and the American regime. An inquiry such as "When you say 'you,' do you mean 'we' the Americans or 'me' the therapist?" may help the Arabic client be aware of the differences between the American government in general and the therapist as a particular person.

As collectivists, Arab/Muslim clients can be helped by a counselor who empathizes with their collective culture. Manisfest acceptance, tolerance, and unconditional positive regard toward the family and tradition on the part of the therapist may help these clients trust him and relinquish anger or inferiority feelings. Empathy and acceptance that is limited to the individual client and does not encompass the family and culture is not enough, and in some cases may be counterproductive or threatening. Empathizing with the client while at the same time pushing her to cope assertively with her family may place her prematurely in an irresolvable conflict.

Western counselors should also be aware of their own countertransference toward Arab/Muslim clients and families. They need to be open to listening and learning about clients and their families and must strip themselves of any stereotypic notions and prejudices that they may have absorbed from the Western media. They may need to make a great conscious effort to avoid judging the clients' and their families' behavior and attitudes according to the Western norms and values.

Collective Psychocultural Features of Arabs/Muslims

Tribalism, Islam, and exposure to the West constitute the main components of the Arab/Muslim collective experience that shaped the Arab/Muslim culture today. Actually, all three components of the collective experience contributed to the submissiveness of Arabs/Muslims to the tribal authority, or to the Islamic teachings, or to Western imperialism. Throughout their long history they have relied, for survival, on a midway collective entity, such as family tribes, clan, or extended family, which mediated between the political authority and the individual. There was no way for the individual to become an independent entity. Individuals are components of the collective that should serve the cohesion and needs of the collective in order to be served by that collective. In this social system two polarized options are open to individuals: (a) to be submissive in order to gain vital collective support, or (b) to relinquish the collective support in favor of self-fulfillment. Arabs/Muslims are spread between these two poles and can be roughly categorized into three categories: authoritarian/collectivists, mixed, and individualistic. The vast majority of Arabs/Muslims are found in the first two categories. Few Arabs/Muslims can be characterized as individualists; those who are were typically raised in educated middle-class families and have been exposed to Western culture. Of course, these categories are dynamic and contextual. Generally speaking, the majority of Arabs/Muslims tend to adopt a collective system of values when dealing with family issues within their homes while they may adopt mixed or individualistic attitudes when dealing with political or economic practices in society. It is not unusual for a father, for instance, to practice traditional attitudes toward his wife and daughters while he is active in a communist or democratic party.

Individuals in a collective society are dependent for their survival on their families; and families' cohesion, economy, status, and reputation are in turn dependent on individuals' behavior and achievements. Individual choices in life are collective matters, and therefore almost all the major decisions in life are determined by the collective. Decisions concerning clothing, social activity, career, marriage, housing, size of the family, and child rearing are taken within the family context where the individual has only a marginal influence. Arranged or forced marriages are very common (see Chapter 5). In some extreme cases, marriage may take place even without asking the opinion of the bride or the bridegroom. Within this system, in which issues are determined by others, the individual learns to be helpless as an individual, avoids personal initiative or challenges, and expects matters to be arranged by some external force. Put in other terms, Arabs/Muslims tend to have an external locus of control (Dwairy, 1998a).

In the collective, social norms and values determine the course of people's life rather than personal decisions, and therefore diversity within such a culture is very limited. People think, feel, and behave according to a priori determined standards. Within the family, it is unusual to find diverse attitudes in social, religious, or political issues. All family members adopt and voice similar attitudes. To maintain the cohesion of the collective system (see Chapter 4), authentic self-expression of feelings is not welcomed; instead, one is expected to express what others anticipate. This way of communication within the collective is directed by values of respect *(ihtiram),* fulfilling social duties *(wajib),* and pleasing others and avoiding confrontations *(mosayara).* Emotional expressions on good or bad occasions, such as marriage or death, are ruled by social norms.

Counselors may misunderstand this dependency of Arab/Muslim clients and misattribute it to immaturity of the self. Counselors are recommended to try to understand the rationale of this dependency and remember that freedom of choice and personal decision making is punishable, even among adults. This caution is crucial when the client is a female, because disobedience may have fatal consequences for her.

SOCIALIZATION, FAMILY STRUCTURE, AND GENDER ROLES

The majority of Arabs/Muslims live in large families. The typical nuclear family consists of parents and five to ten children. The nuclear family is typically not independent but is enmeshed within the extended patriarchic family *(hamula or ashira)* that includes three or more generations of the father's family. Sometimes the nuclear family shares the budget with the extended family, the grandfather managing the economics of the family and the grandmother managing the household and child rearing. Frequently they live in a shared complex or neighborhood. Privacy is nonexistent and everybody intervenes in everybody's affairs. In return, nuclear families enjoy the emotional, social, and economic support and help of the extended family. Within this system the role of the males is to manage the family property and to earn money, while that of the females is to run the household and take care of the children. Within this system there are two separate societies, one for men and another for women. The contact between the two is limited and task oriented (Barakat, 2000). In the last few decades, however, especially in the cities and among educated people, this interdependence within the extended families has been weakened ('Authman, 1999).

Rearing and socialization of children in a collective society also tends to be authoritarian, to foster collective values such as submissiveness, and to educate for sacrifice of the self and for the cohesion and interest of the family. Despite diversity in child rearing methods and socialization in the Arab/Muslim family, one can find a general common pattern that is more explicit among traditional families. Parents control their children's behavior and allow them little room for freedom of choice. Initially, they use verbal measures such as guidance, directives, and advice. Typically, these directives are not limited to what the child should do, but also include warnings and threats of punishment in case of disobedience. If these measures do not succeed, parents immediately move to a combination of deprivation and corporal punishment, on the one hand, and belittling, moralizing, and shaming, on the other. The move from verbal guidance to deprivation and punishment is made regardless of the issue with which they are dealing. In one study I conducted among Arab/Muslim parents, the subjects presented their two-stage plan of verbal admonition followed by punishments as their solution for every problem about which they were asked (Dwairy, 1998a). Both mothers and fathers adopt this plan to control their male and female children. Only minor differences were found between the plans of fathers and mothers, and between the treatment of boys and girls. Although both parents support the same plan, mothers, being closer to the children, tend to try to mitigate the punishment, expressing some degree of empathic affection for the child or dissatisfaction with the punishment, while fathers tend to be more remote and stricter, displaying less affection. Mothers tend to be ambivalent: They express a lot of positive affection, but conversely express weariness with the burden they carry, and sometimes helplessness. Mothers serve as buffers between the patriarchal authority and their children: They often play the role of the weak agent obliged to fulfill the will of the stronger patriarchal authority, but they also threaten the children with the father's authority when they disobey. Mothers use sentences such as "I will tell your father when he returns home" on a daily basis. These women's attitudes in fact maintain the patriarchical system.

Both Arab/Muslim mothers and fathers address the conscience of the child through moralization, but mothers do so with deeper feeling and more affection. Despite the large "meal" of moralization the children have to digest, more has been written about shame rather than guilt feelings as directing the behavior of Arabs/Muslims. Shame is an external locus of control (that is related to the self-respect value mentioned above) and guilt is an internal locus that has to do with a developed conscience. In fact, although shame is a dominant feeling in the Arab/Muslim life, guilt feelings are also dominant within the family relationship, especially in the relationship with the mother or any other entities that are metaphorically associated with the mother in the Arab/Muslim culture, such as the land or homeland (Barakat, 1993, 2000). Because of the differences in the parental roles, the child's attitudes toward the father are characterized by respect and even fear, while attitudes toward the mother are characterized by love, affection, and guilt (Patai, 2002). Although there are qualitative differences in the issues that may provoke the guilt feelings of Arabs/Muslims compared to Westerners, it would be a mistake to consider the Arab/Muslim conscience to be less developed or less active. In fact, the main difference between the two cultures may be in the dominance of shame rather than of guilt. As a result of psychological individuation in the West, shame has become less dominant than it is among Arabs/Muslims, who adopt a collective conscience and remain dependent on relationships with others.

Arab/Muslim schools adopt authoritarian educational means, too. Teachers expect students to memorize information. They allow limited space for dialogue and critical thinking. They do not encourage initiative or creativity. Corporal punishment is common in Arab/Muslim schools. Parents do not oppose, even if some of them do not justify, these means. The major functions that students learn at schools are to memorize and to follow directives and orders, on the one hand, and to be detached from their own feelings and avoid self-expression, on the other (Dwairy, 1997c).

Parenting Styles

The authoritarian parenting style is considered in the West to be a negative style that does not promote the mental health of children. However, it seems that the authoritarian style has a different effect on Arab/Muslim children. In research that was intended to study the socialization measures that Arab/Muslim parents use in the upbringing of their adolescent children, it was found, as expected, that the parents are very controlling. Interestingly, Arab/Muslim adolescents seem accepting of that control without consistent complaint (Hatab & Makki, 1978). In a study on violence in Arab schools, students reported the frequent verbal and physical punishments that teachers apply, but the amount of complaints that students expressed was not proportional, as if they accept that treating students in that way is a natural part of the teacher's role (Dwairy, 1997c). There is more than a hint that the authoritarian parenting style does not impair the mental health of Arab/Muslim children as it does that of their Western counterparts. When the relationship between parenting styles (authoritarian, authoritative, and permissive) and the psychological adjustment of Arab/Muslim youth was studied, a positive correlation was found between the authoritative style and several measures of psychological adjustment such as self-concept and self-esteem, and a negative correlation with anxiety, depression, and behavior disorders. No significant correlation at all was found between the authoritarian style and any measure of psychological maladjustment, suggesting that the authoritarian parenting style does not impair the mental health of Arab/Muslim adolescents (Dwairy, Achoui, Abouserie, & Farah, in press).

Generally speaking, the authoritarian parenting style of Arabs/Muslims is stricter in relation to girls than to boys. For girls, limits and prohibitions become stricter when they reach adolescence. Their space becomes limited to the house and their relationships to females within the household of the family and a few other carefully screened girls. They are asked to take responsibilities in the household, such as cleaning and arranging the house and preparing food. Actually, they are preparing for their foreclosed future role as wives and mothers. They have limited choices and many of them are obliged to marry a husband of the family's choice. Sometimes the two families of the bride and the bridegroom arrange the marriage (Dwairy, 1998a). Arab females identify with the familial authority. In a study of their attitudes, it was found that two thirds of female (and one third of male) college students in Egypt supported "full adherence" to the parents' wishes (Al-Khawaja, 1999). This adherence may indicate girls' identification with the authoritarian parenting and may explain why they complain less about authoritarian parenting than do boys (Dwairy, 2004e, 2004d).

Implications for Counselors

Counselors who work with Arab/Muslim clients should bear in mind that the intrapsychic constructs such as self, ego, and superego are not independent constructs but rather are collective structures that include the collective norms and values. Counselors are directed to give more attention to intrafamilial conflicts and coalitions than to intrapsychic processes within the individual client. Western counselors may find it difficult to understand the rationale of the authoritarian parenting style since they have not experienced for themselves (as Arabs/Muslims have) the vital individual-family interdependence that exists where state-provided care is absent. Counselors may easily find themselves opposing the authority of the Arab/Muslim families and employing therapeutic and legal means to create liberal egalitarian order in the family. Imposing such Western values on Arab/Muslim families is, however, both unethical and counterproductive. Instead, counselors are encouraged to try to understand the rationale of the authoritarian system from within, to listen to the stresses and anxieties that the authoritarian parents experience, to express empathy for their conflicts, and to encourage and empower those progressive components in the parents' value system that may facilitate therapeutic changes. Counselors should consider their role to be serving the needs of the client within his or her family and value system rather than imposing their own needs and values on the client. Besides, threatening the familial authority might terminate the counseling process and leave the client to suffer the consequences.

Emigration to the West exposes and challenges all the cultural features mentioned in this chapter. Before and after emigration, a fundamental cultural revision and change takes place in the mind of the Arab/Muslim. The Western liberal/individualistic life may seem too permissive and therefore may threaten traditional Arab/Muslim values concerning family, women, and child rearing. At some stage, emigrants may become aware of and committed to some Arab/Muslim cultural norms and values that were marginal before emigration. They may find refuge in their culture of origin to avoid the confusion that takes place in their lives as a result of moving to a new society toward which they may already have an ambivalent attitude. The next chapter will address the cultural status of Arab/Muslim emigrants in the West.

SUMMARY

Tribalism, Islam, and exposure to the West have shaped the collective culture of Arabs/Muslims. Social norms and values determine the people's behavior rather than personal decisions. The choices that individuals face are between submissiveness in order to gain vital familial support and relinquishing the support in favor of self-fulfillment. Counselors need to be aware of the diversity among Arabs/Muslims that is generated by local influences, modernization, and urbanization.

Chapter 3

Arab/Muslim Families in the United States

KHAWLA ABU-BAKER

Historically, the development of the identity of Arabs living in the United States has been influenced by many factors: (a) the reason for migration; (b) the type of relationship developed with mainstream Americans; (c) the official stance of American legislation toward Arab immigrants; (d) political developments in the Middle East; (e) the Islamic revolution in Iran (Abraham, 1983; Naff, 1983, 1985); and, most recently, (f) the terrorist events of September 11, 2001 (Bonnie & Hasan, 2004; Ibish, 2003; Zogby, 2001). Some of these factors reflect the interrelationship between immigrants and the American context, while others reflect the relationship between immigrants and the Middle Eastern context.

Very little has been written about the mental health of Arab immigrants in the United States (Abudabbeh, 1996; Abudabbeh & Nydell, 1993; Meleis, 1981; Meleis & La Fever, 1984). However, it is believed that Arab Americans as a group, are misunderstood, misrepresented, and stereotyped (Jackson, 1997; Suleiman, 1988), with the result that they do not receive the right treatment in therapy (Erickson & Al-Tamimi, 2001).

CURRENT DEMOGRAPHICS

The census of 2000 indicated that about 3.5 million Americans are of Arab descent. Also according to the census data, more than 80% of Arabs are U.S. citizens and 63% were born in the United States (El-Badry, 1994; Arab American Institute [AAI], 2005). Half the Arab immigrants are Christian and half are Muslim (AAI, 2005).

It is estimated that there are 8.5 million Muslims in America (Institute of Islamic Information and Education, 2005). While Arabs immigrated from the Middle East, Muslims immigrated from about 80 different countries. Unlike Arabs, non-Arab Muslims belong to a variety of ethnic groups and nations, originating mostly in South Asia, Indonesia, and Iran. Thus they speak many different languages. The first immigrant Muslims arrived in America as slaves from Africa. The reasons for the recent mass Muslim immigration are: (a) ethnic persecution, such as in Uganda, Tanzania, and Kenya; (b) religious persecution, such as the Hindu-Muslim conflicts in India; (c) Islamism, such as in Iran, Sudan, and Pakistan; (d) anti-Islamism, in countries where the lives of individuals and groups are threatened by extremists; and (e) civil wars, such as in former Yugoslavia (Pipes & Duran, 2002).

Although concentrated in 11 states, Arabs live in all 50 states; however, the overwhelming majority, about 94%, live in major metropolitan areas such as Washington, D.C., New York, Chicago, Los Angeles, and Detroit. The Arab Americans are younger than any other ethnic group, with more than 30% of the whole population being under 18 years old. They are among the more highly educated immigrants: 40% of the Arab American population have at least a bachelor's degree, and 17% have a postgraduate degree. These percentages are twice those found among the American population as a whole. The average income of Arabs is higher than the American average ($47,000 per annum compared to $42,000). Most of the adults, about 64%, are part of the labor force: 88% work in the private sector, and the rest are government employees. However, Arabs tend to hold different occupations in different cities. El-Badry (1994) found that among those who reside in Washington, D.C., and Anaheim, California, 23% are executives, while 18% of Houston's Arab residents are professionals. Cleveland's Arab residents work mainly in sales; in Bergen-Passaic, New Jersey, and in New York City the emphasis is on administrative jobs.

THE WAVES OF IMMIGRATION

By the end of the nineteenth century, Arabs had started to immigrate to the United States, driven by curiosity, a sense of adventure, famine, political events, and religious and cultural considerations (Naff, 1985). The course of their immigration is divided into three major waves which took place over a period of about a century.

1. The first wave, from 1880–1914, consisted mainly of Christians, who emigrated from what is now Syria and Lebanon for political, economic, and religious reasons (Kayal, 1983; Khalaf, 1987; Naff, 1985). This group integrated into the mainstream society and economy. They westernized their names, learned English, and adopted the American lifestyle (Halaby, 1987; Suleiman, 1987).
2. The second wave started immediately after the 1948 war and the establishment of Israel and continued until the 1960s. Subsequently, each war

in the Middle East caused an increase in Arab immigration to the United States. These immigrants made their ethnic and political identity their main concern (Zogby, 1990), preferring to reside in "Arab ethnic ghettos" where several Arab families lived in the same building or neighborhood. This wave created concentrated Arab neighborhoods such as in Dearborn, Michigan, where the immigrants tried to duplicate the natural life of their home countries (A. Farag, personal communication, February 1997).

3. The third wave started after the Arab defeat in the 1967 war between Israel and the Arab world and came to a halt after September 11, 2001. These immigrants were escaping political instability and searching for better economic opportunities (Abraham, 1995; Naff, 1983). The last immigrants to arrive in the United States as a national group consisted of Iraqi immigrants from Iraq after the Iraqi-Iranian war in the 1980s and the Gulf war in the mid-1990s (Kira, 1999). In comparison with other immigrants and the regular population, this group of immigrants suffered from a high rate of depression, anxiety, post-traumatic stress disorder (PTSD), and substance abuse, as well as a high rate of somatization (Jamil et al., 2002).

The First Wave

Ninety per cent of the first wave of immigrants were Christian. Living in the Arab world, Christians were typical Middle Eastern people, whose traditions and culture were very similar to that of the Muslim population. However, they were distinguished by their religious, economic, and political links with the West, as a result of their openness to the Christian civilization, especially in Italy, Greece, and France (Kayal, 1983). During the Ottoman era, they were discriminated against as a religious minority; moreover, they were sought out and massacred in some villages. After the year 1850, Arabs developed an unrealistic picture of the wealth of the new countries in the Americas from stories told by European merchants (Suleiman, 1987) and by a few Arab immigrants who returned home to tell about their adventures. The Chicago fair held in 1893 and that of Saint Louis in 1906 also encouraged merchants and others to migrate (Khalaf, 1987). In migration, the educated and intellectual groups found an escape from the repressive political atmospheres.

Christian peasants, merchants, and intellectuals from Syria and Lebanon started arriving in America in 1869 at the rate of 2 persons a year; by 1913 the rate of immigration had risen to about 9,200 persons a year (Khalaf, 1987). The motive of those who fled their country of origin for economic reasons was to amass wealth in the United States and return home. As the economic and political situation in their homeland worsened due to high taxes and conscription in the army of the Ottomans, Christians and Muslims considered immigration as a solution for all their problems (Kayal, 1983; Naff, 1985). Today, immigrants from Syria, Lebanon, and Palestine make up the majority of immigrants from Arab countries; however, all Arab countries are represented in the mosaic of Arab immigrants (McCarus, 1994; AAI, 2005).

In the Middle East, Islam is a lifestyle for Arab individuals (Abu-Baker, in press; Lovel, 1983; Patai, 1983). However, many Arabs, especially the Christians, grasp the depth of the influence of Islam on their daily life only after they immigrate. Then they become more traditional and/or religious than they used to be in their home country. This tendency is a reaction to the intense influences of the acculturation they experience. They try to reflect their appreciation of their own norms by focusing on maintaining the traditional structure of the family. Arab families are expected to treat parents with sacred respect and revere their elders and take care of them when in need; they expect unchallenged obedience from women and children, abstain from sex outside wedlock, and maintain segregation between the sexes. The main building block of society is the family, not the individual. Arabs identify themselves by their ties to their extended families, who are expected to provide all economic, political, social, and psychological support to their members. In this kind of family, individuals are required to put the family's interest before their own, and when they do not, they either are accused of selfishness or struggle with self-blame.

Most of the first immigrants were men. Lebanese immigrants tended to go back to Lebanon to marry and return to the United States with their wives. Immigrants from other Arab countries remained unmarried for the most part, especially Muslims who found it difficult to marry Christian women because of religious intolerance and the local attitudes against the Middle Eastern immigrant group (Bilgé & Aswad, 1996). The 1990 census data indicate that 54% of Arabs in America are men, compared to 49% of the total U.S. population (El-Badry, 1994).

While in the Middle East, Christians survived as a minority by virtue of nurturing their congregations. In the United States, with its Protestant majority, orthodox Christians once more felt that they were in the minority. As a result of their small number, Syrian Eastern Orthodox assimilated with Roman Catholics. Also Malketes and Maronites, who belonged to the Eastern Orthodox Church, surrendered their autonomy to the Roman Catholic Church. In some cases, Syrian Eastern Orthodox established some parishes with other immigrants from Greece and Russia. Very few ethnic Eastern parishes exist today in the United States (Kayal, 1983).

Later Waves

The second wave of immigrants emphasized their nationalism rather than their religion. This immigration occurred immediately after World War II, which, together with the establishment of Israel in 1948, caused turmoil in the Arab world. Palestinian immigrants who were forced into exile from their homeland sought to immigrate to the United States. Other groups from Egypt, Lebanon, Syria, Yemen, and Iraq immigrated for political, economic, and mobility reasons. These groups were composed of people who already had capital and college degrees or wanted to acquire them. They were ethnically conscious and politically vocal, a tendency that helped them gradually to become a visible minority in the United States (Zogby, 1990).

The difference in the ethnic and political conscience of each wave of immigrants reflects the change in the geopolitical map in the Arab World. For example, at the time of the first wave of immigration, Arab countries were ruled by Ottomans, who were Muslims but not Arabs. Thus they encouraged an Islamic identity rather than a nationalist one, since they themselves were a minority in the region. During World War I, the political map of the Arab World changed and with it the borders of some countries. For example, people who lived in what is known today as Syria and Lebanon all called themselves Syrians during the Ottoman period. After the British and French occupation of and mandate over the area, what is known today as Syria, Lebanon, and Israel was called Larger Syria (Kayal, 1983). After World War II, Arab countries gained their independence from foreign regimes and soon national and pan-Arab movements emerged. A new sociopolitical Arab identity developed, especially in Egypt, under the leadership of Gamal Abdel Nasser. People who migrated to the United States after this period came with a crystallized ethnopolitical identity (Abraham, 1983; Abraham, Abraham, & Aswad, 1983; Naff, 1983).

THE ENCOUNTER WITH THE AMERICAN SYSTEM

When Arab individuals immigrate to improve their own individual life conditions, they are expected to support other family members who follow in their footsteps.

In one example, Fareed, a garage mechanic, summarized the circumstances that influenced his decision to immigrate:

> Everything went wrong. After 1967 you could not find good jobs [in Jordan] because of the Palestinian refugees who had been expelled from the West Bank. The doors were closed in my face. I worked for 15 hours a day, but by the end of the month I had no money to feed my children. Then I realized that I had no way to make a living in my country. I decided to follow my brother Shareef, who has become a rich professor in America.

Thus Fareed followed his brother Shareef to the United States, following the pattern of Arab immigration whereby a "family chain" is formed. The already settled immigrants help settle their relatives and friends and people from the same village or neighborhood, who in turn help other friends and relatives. This pattern of migration was established by the first wave of immigrants, who settled in communities with village and religious ties, restructuring some of their homeland relationships (Abraham, Abraham, & Aswad, 1983; Conklin & Faires, 1987; Naff, 1985).

After immigration, Arabs seek to live in communities with other Arabs. However, they work within the American system and send their children to American schools, both public and private. These encounters create challenges for individuals and tension within families. Regarding mastery of culture and language, the immigrants may be divided into two major groups: the academic immigrants who are more acquainted with American culture and language, and the workers who for the most part ignore both. Daily life in America seems so strange and different from life in the societies of origin that many parents minimize their encounter with the social life of the Americans.

Some of the problems that face Arabs and Muslims in the United States relate to the fact that they are now living in a non-Islamic country. Many Islamic religious laws and restrictions do not suit the rhythm of American daily life. For instance, Muslims have to pray five times daily at prescribed times; religious Muslims find it difficult when schools and workplaces do not consider this need. Another important issue is the Islamic dietary laws which forbid the consumption of pork and alcohol, and all foods containing them; eating improperly slaughtered meat is also forbidden (Haddad, 1983). Economically, religious Muslims abstain from receiving loans on which they have to pay interest, since this is considered a sin in Islam; thus they are not able to buy houses or start new businesses in the United States because they are not able to borrow interest-free money (Noorzoy, 1983). Finally, adult Muslim women have to observe a strict, modest dress code. They cover their body in accordance with the degree of their religious fundamentalism and their traditional background (Haddad, 1983).

From the mental health point of view, many aspects of the encounter with the American system cause stress; some of these issues will be discussed in the following sections.

Difficulties with the Language

When they arrive in the United States, even educated people find the effort to master the English language and the American dialect, as most Americans expect foreigners to do, very stressful. Many people therefore feel handicapped and experience a decrease in their self-esteem, something they had never experienced in their home country. In their country of origin they had been perceived by themselves and others as experts in English. People who fail to learn English in the United States are unable to acquire a driver's license, since they cannot understand the written exam or read the street signs. They are also unable to understand American TV or answer phone calls or use the phone to arrange their business. Those who do not know the language are not able to read the ingredients on the merchandise. Failure to master the language will lead to failure in the citizenship test, causing the family's expulsion from the country. Their degree of mastery of the English language determines whether Arab workers are able to work directly with Americans or not (for instance, working in the kitchen or with clients in a restaurant). For women who have no previous knowledge of English, this ignorance leads to isolation from American life, to being closed within the Arab cultural ghetto, and to total dependence on husband and children in all encounters with the host country. For immigrants, therefore, proficiency in English is the first step toward regaining self-esteem and experiencing relief from the continuous tension. English is also needed for communication purposes, for passing the citizenship test, and for maintaining an active life. Although the work environment may enable the immigrant to learn the language, most immigrants think that they have to master the language before progressing further.

Legal Status

Before September 11, 2001, many Arab/Muslim immigrants arrived in America on a tourist visa, decided to stay, and then had to try to gain legal status. Lack of legal status influences the mental health of the illegal immigrant families and their families back home, as well as the type of work adults may do. Subsequently, it impacts the families' lifestyle and well-being. Most illegal immigrants moved to America to join other family members, friends, or relatives. A few Arab immigrants use marriage, either real or fictitious, to gain permanent status in the country. Others pay immigration lawyers substantial amounts to gain permission to work and attain permanent status. When illegal immigrants marry women from other Arab countries, these wives live in the United States as illegal citizens. They are not allowed to give their husbands or children the right to citizenship status in their home countries. In cases where abusive husbands divorce their wives against their will (a religious ceremony which is not filed in the American system) and kidnap their children, these women are left without any ability to file complaints to the authorities against the ex-husbands, since they lack legal citizenship. In other cases, parents leave some or all of their children in their home country to convince the authorities to issue a tourist visa to the United States. Upon their arrival in America, they start trying to gain their permanent status. A couple who arrived with their 3-year-old boy has not been able to see the daughter, who was 10 months old when they left her behind in their home country, for the last 4 years. Meanwhile, they both work to cover legal expenses. Many illegal immigrants live with the feeling of being besieged; since they would not be able to reenter the United States, they are unable to visit their home country, sometimes for the rest of their lives.

Work

Illegal Arab/Muslim immigrants are not able to find jobs in their professions since they lack the proper documents. This causes a lessening of their social and professional status. They are forced to work in the family business and accept minimum wages. As a direct result, they have to work an average of 15 hours a day, which in turn creates family tension and frustration. On the other hand, wives who are left alone with their children feel lonely and frustrated, and lose the sense of companionship in their marriages.

Families who immigrate gradually as nuclear families and then gather together in the United States as an extended family establish family businesses into which several brothers and/or brothers-in-law invest all their collective capital and divide the labor among themselves. In cases where the business succeeds, all family members benefit from the common effort and the family-based business. However, when all the adults are experiencing severe tension caused by the immigration adjustment, working together becomes an emotionally charged activity. In cases of financial problems, such as crippling debts or business bankruptcy, all extended family members suffer without having an outside safety net.

Social Status

Survival needs in the host country often force immigrants to work in jobs very different from their professional training, a situation which deprives them of the social status they had in their homeland. These people feel ashamed and humiliated by the work they do. In order to save face, they prefer to reframe the type of jobs they do, telling others that they work as a "supermarket manager" or a "business accountant," respectful professions that enable immigrants to claim a higher status. One couple who immigrated to the United States in the hope of curing the wife's infertility was very rich and had belonged to the upper class in Jordan. Back home the husband had worked as an airplane mechanic; in the United States the only work he could find was in a grocery store. The wife had been a high school teacher in Jordan, but in the United States became a baby sitter, helping with the housekeeping. Both concealed their jobs from their family of origin in Jordan.

Anonymity in America is a psychological as well as a social situation which is alien to the traditional lifestyle in small communities in the Arab countries; there it is enough to mention one's last name to gain respect and preferential treatment, while in the United States one must follow another path to better social status, such as education, work, and wealth. For example, two sisters, who belonged to a sacred clan in Morocco with genealogy going back to the prophet Mohammad, were frustrated by the fact that in the United States they belonged to the lower class. Poor immigrant Arab men asked for their hands in marriage, making them feel that they had been deprived of their former social status. They were told, "If you want to stay here, you have to understand the new social conditions; otherwise, go back home."

Although the standard of living in America is much higher than in most countries in the Middle East, people measure themselves by both their social status back home and their actual social status in America. Whether their status is legal or not, in the first few years in their new country immigrants may feel a decrease in their social status that affects their mental health. Career women in particular feel the status change and suffer deeply from it. They are not able to work in grocery stores as men do. And usually they have small children whom they cannot put in day care because they do not have the financial ability.

Families who live in poor neighborhoods and send their children to public school often prohibit their children from socializing with other American children, because they believe that poor Americans have very low social values that may influence Arab children, leaving them with bad manners.

Social Life

The structure of the family's relationships, the type of work the adults do, and the distance between households all determine the type of social life a family enjoys. Arab people in the Middle East have a very tightly knit social life. They often meet with family members and neighbors on a daily basis. In the United States it is difficult to continue this custom because of the long distances and protracted work hours. Arab children are completely isolated from peer social life and from after-school activities. Arabs therefore look for ways to meet more often, such as moving to live together in the same neighborhood and meeting at an Islamic center once a week for daylong activities. Extended families who immigrate together face fewer problems regarding their social life than others, and their children keep each other company. The individualistic lifestyle is very strange to the interdependent Arab society. In America, Arabs see the lack of an active social life as a personal failure, since individuals who keep themselves aloof from social life are believed to have psychological problems. Loneliness is the primary feeling described by women who immigrated without their extended families, especially during the first year.

Moslem women who take their children to an Islamic center to learn Arabic and religion meet each Saturday for about 4 to 6 hours. Women tend to socialize in accordance with family or regional ties. For many women, especially those who live within extended families, the weekly visit to the Islamic center is the only social activity they have to enjoy. Other immigrants may find a refuge for social meetings in Arab organizations, clubs, or societies. Such organizations organize cultural events and invite singers and lecturers from the Arab world.

Part of the social life of Arab immigrants is accepting guests from their home countries as visitors. The average duration of each visit varies between 2 weeks and 3 months, while some guests may stay up to 6 months. During such visits all their friends in the community pay visits to the family and invite them with their guest to a feast. These visits are opportunities to refresh the children's Arabic language, norms, and values.

Tension Between Spouses

Women who immigrate from the Middle East or other Muslim countries to marry immigrant men have high expectations of living in the United States. However, when these couples face the real challenges involved, most women feel betrayed. They look to their husbands to fulfill their promises of a dream life in America. Couples who immigrated according to a mutual decision share their immigration problems better than others because the immigration challenges become a family project that the couple has to work on together. A major problem is the long hours the husband, or both husband and wife, must invest in their new jobs and new responsibilities, which leave them with no energy or time to support each other as a couple.

Inhibition of Interfaith or Intercultural Marriages

Parents control their teenage children's behavior and relations, discouraging social or intimate relations with non-Arabs. Even Christian Arabs who felt themselves to be a minority in the Middle East feel more Arab than Christian in the United States. This group also prefers their children to marry Arab rather than non-Arab Christians. Marriage between Arab Muslims and non-Arab Muslims (Indian or Chinese for instance) is also discouraged. Religious centers and Arab organizations offer opportunities for parents and individuals to look for a good matrimonial match. With all the restrictions that exist, it is more often that Arab men marry outside the faith and culture than Arab women.

Teenagers

Teenagers who try to imitate their American peers face constant correction of their conduct; parents try to efface all non-Arab behaviors and norms. Boys and girls experience ongoing arguments with their parents regarding their rights, especially when they compare themselves with American teenagers. In response, parents forbid any out-of-classroom encounters with American children in an attempt to minimize the influence of American culture on them (Barazangi, 1996; Swanson, 1996). Furthermore, they send their children to Islamic centers or to Christian Arab congregations to learn Arabic and religion, either on a daily basis or for a few concentrated hours on weekends. Parents, community centers, and religious centers are enlisted to help isolate children from American culture and to influence their socialization in congruence with the ethos of Arabic and Islamic cultures. An ultimate tool parents use to control teenagers who rebel against their norms is sending them back to their extended family in their homeland for an unlimited time to "fix" their behavior. To persuade young Muslims to marry within the faith, parents send their children to their home countries to meet their relatives almost every summer, and encourage socializing in the Islamic centers and summer camps. In addition, imams mediate between single men and women; and the community encourages marriage advertisements.

THE COLLECTIVE SELF

External events in the Middle East, internal events and the experiences of Arab immigrants during the process of acculturation, and political events in the world all combine to form the self-identity of Arabs in America. The sense of a collective self has undergone a major shift since the terrorist attack on the United States in 2001 by Bin Laden's followers, and is reflected in the activities of Arab organizations.

Before September 11, 2001

People who immigrated from what is known today as Syria and Lebanon were called by immigration authorities either Syrian, Turk, Ottoman, or Armenian (Khalaf, 1987; Suleiman, 1988). After World War I, immigrants of the first wave debated whether to go back "home" or to make America "home." Some Arab voices started writing, in their established newspapers, about the necessity to assimilate and stop living, behaving, and feeling as outsiders of the American society (Halaby, 1987; Suleiman, 1987, 1994). Arabs started expressing and discussing their suffering regarding the American mainstream rejection and discrimination against them (Conklin & Faires, 1987; Halaby, 1987). Abraham (1995), Fa'ik (1994), Halaby (1987), Nobles and Sciarra (2000), and Stockton (1994) highlight the discrimination, stereotyping, and prejudice that were established and expanded by the American media against Arabs and Muslims. The broken English and poor appearance of the pioneer Arab pack peddlers in the late nineteenth century, and the Arab-Israeli wars in the twentieth century are some of the main reasons for the rapidly growing prejudice.

After World War I, Arabs, feeling rejected by and isolated from the American institutions and mainstream citizens, started to reconstruct their own ethnoreligious institutions. The Christians established parishes and organizations on the basis of religious affiliation. They also founded institutions, mainly on the basis of homeland geopolitical gathering (Kayal, 1983). Arab media always prospered among Arab immigrants. Between 1898 and 1929, a total of 102 Arabic-language newspapers and periodicals came into existence, but few have survived. Some English-language newspapers also developed, serving second generation immigrants (Halaby, 1987). These newspapers helped connect immigrants to events in the Middle East and influenced the Arabs living in the West to maintain the Arabic language, to discuss the communities' concerns, and to criticize Arab or Western politics. It is common today to find Arab newspapers divided into two sections, one in Arabic and another in English, addressing the different needs of the community.

After the 1967 war between Israel and the Arab countries, large numbers of highly politicized immigrants arrived in the United States. They soon established their own newspapers, magazines, and television and radio shows. Arabic theaters for adults and for children were also established (Halaby, 1987). The goal of this wave of media and theater was to teach, crystallize, and maintain Arab identity in America among Muslim and Christian immigrants.

Barazangi's (1996) research conclusions about the identity of Arabs in North America showed that 82% of the parents in the sample identified themselves mainly with their home country. Eleven percent identified themselves with pan-Arabism notions, and 6% with Islam. When the interviewees were asked how they introduce their identity to non-Muslims, 11% answered "Arab"; the majority answered "American"; and no one answered "Muslim." When children were asked about their identity, 35% identified themselves as being of Arab origin and 29% as Muslim; 18% identified themselves with their home country; and 18% responded "none of the above."

Despite the fact that Arab people in the United States identify themselves as Arabs, "Awlad ʿArab-Children of Arabs," or by the country they migrated from, such as Syrians or Lebanese (Kayal, 1983; Naff, 1985), political and community leaders coined the concept "Arab American" in the early 1980s, which identified all immigrants from the Arab-speaking world. Many organizations have been established around the concept (Zogby, 1990).

Arab identity in America was also influenced by their rejection by American mainstream society. As a result of the media's evoking stereotypes against Arabs and Muslims in the United States, especially after World War II (Abraham, 1995; Bilgé & Aswad, 1996; Stockton, 1994), Arab immigrants were marginalized from political and social integration into the mainstream of society. They soon realized that the only way to exist was within cultural and/or physical ghettos. This reaction was strengthened by family and community life in most

Islamic and Arab groups (Abraham, 1983). Muslims started utilizing functions of Islamic institutions such as mosques and Islamic centers for teaching the Arabic language and the religion of Islam. Immigrants from previous generations also supported this tendency (Haddad, 1983).

After September 11, 2001

Arabs and Muslims have reported an increase in prejudice and discrimination encounters with white Americans since September 11, 2001, a new circumstance which has had a direct influence on their self-esteem and mental health. Arab women who wear traditional dress have become afraid to appear veiled in public. Some Arabs were hurt by what were recognized as "hate crimes" (Ibish, 2003; Zogby, 2001). Immediately after the attack on the World Trade Center, Arab Americans expressed their worry about the discrimination against them, and reported that they or others whom they knew had experienced the discrimination directly (Zogby, 2001). It was reported by the Arab American Anti-Discrimination Committee (ADC) that 700 violent acts were committed against Arabs during the 2 months after September 11. The succeeding year the ADC reported a 400% increase in employment discrimination. After analysis of prejudice research literature, Bonnie and Hasan (2004) concluded that a mediated relation between psychological distress and discrimination experiences exists. In their study, they found that 53% of the sample was treated in a discriminatory manner for being of Arab descent; 47% experienced racism against them; while 46% experienced being called racist names. The researchers concluded that it is important for therapists who work with Arab clients to be aware of the effect of discrimination on psychological well-being and to find ways to ease the situation, either in the clinic or via the proper organizations.

Arab Organizations

Since the attack in 2001, Arabs and Muslims in the United States have understood that they have to change the prejudices against them. To reach that goal they are using religious, national, ethnic, professional, and political Arab and/or Islamic organizations, professional Web sites dedicated to introducing Arabs or Islam in a positive manner, and Arab satellite TV stations broadcasting in English for the American audience.

These organizations have a long history; Arabs learned long ago that the best way to face the sociopolitical life in the United States is as a group via organizations. This tendency was responsible for the shift from a guiding principle of self-imposed distancing from the host country to a strategy of participating as equal citizens. Various ethnic religious organizations were established to organize the meeting of immigrants under the same roof. An Islamic association was established in Highland Park, Michigan, in 1919 and in Detroit, Michigan, in 1922. The Young Men's Muslim Association was established in Brooklyn, New York, in 1923, and the Arab Banner Society in Quincy, Massachusetts, in 1930. The first mosques were built in Detroit in 1919 (Abraham, 1983), in North Dakota in 1920, and in Cedar Rapids, Iowa, in 1934. In 1954 the Islamic Center of Washington, D.C., was opened to serve Muslims who resided in the area, as well as Muslim diplomatic corps who lived and worked in the capital (Haddad, 1983). In 1983 Haddad estimated that there were about 400 mosques and Islamic associations in the United States, while 8 years later Pristin and Dart's (1991) estimate was between 600 and 900 mosques. Haddad explains the source of the mosques: "Because Islam does not have a hierarchical structure in which organization is imposed from above, these institutions were of necessity begun by individuals at the local level; participation in them remains optional" (p. 68).

Among other organizations, there are those established by Muslim students such as the Federation of Islamic Associations (FIA), which emphasizes the pan-Arab notion that rejected the religious divisions among Arabs, since its ideological essence emphasized the Arab nationality over other kinds of identities, such as citizenship or religion. The Muslim World League began in Mecca, Saudi Arabia; however, since 1974 it has served as a nongovernmental representative in the United Nations and consultant to UNICEF and UNESCO. All organizations and associations work toward propagating Islam (*da'wah*), publishing Islamic magazines and studies, organizing and sponsoring conferences, organizing pilgrimages (*haj*) to Mecca, sponsoring the building of new mosques, and maintaining the salaries of the religious leaders (imams) brought to the United States from the Arab world (Haddad, 1983). After Protestantism, Catholicism, and Judaism, Bilgé and Aswad (1996) believe that Islam is becoming a significant fourth religion in the United States. It is important to conceive of all the above organizations as components of the support system, established by previous immigrants to foster identity and provide sociocultural needs for themselves and future immigrants.

Since 1967, several national Arab American organizations have been established, mainly by founders who came with the second wave. These organizations served as political movements and "created a cultural bond across the immigrant generations" (Zogby, 1990, p. ix). Among these organizations are the National Association of Arab Americans (NAAA), the Arab American Anti-Discrimination Committee (ADC), and the Arab American Institute (AAI). There are also several national professional organizations such as the Arab American Medical Association (AAMA) and Arab American Business and Profession Association (AABPA). A wider list of Islamic organization in the United States is available in Waugh, Abu-Laban, and Qureshi (1983). Since September 11, 2001 organizations in the United States and in the Arab World try to ameliorate their reputation and role both in the United States and around the world.

SUMMARY

Arabs and Muslims immigrated to the United States as a result of political and economic reasons. In the host country, they faced social, political, and economic difficulties such as English language proficiency, alienation with the new life-style, disrespect of Arab/Muslim women's dress code, psychological and social stress as a result of American individualism and family norms. Except for the first wave of immigrants, all others tried to maintain geographical and cultural ghettos. This solution helped Arab/Muslim immigrants mutually support each other socially and psychologically. On the other hand, it created isolation from the American mainstream, a tendency that fertilized the ground for stereotypes and hatred to spring up gradually against them, reaching a peak after September 11, 2001. Organizations and Islamic centers play a substantial role in enhancing families' welfare and the legal status of Arab/Muslim communities.

PART II

REVISING WESTERN THEORIES OF DEVELOPMENT AND PERSONALITY

How does exposure to collective/authoritarian culture influence the psychosocial development, personality, and psychopathology of Arabs/Muslims? Reading Chapters 4–6, Western practitioners will begin to realize that some of the well-established notions incoporated in theories of development and personality need to be revised in order to understand Arab/Muslim immigrants and avoid pathologization of their emotions, attitudes, and behavior. Independence of the self and the distinctions between mind and body and between the individual and the family are some of the major notions that need to be reconsidered when working with Arabs/Muslims.

These cross-cultural differences render a culturally sensitive approach to assessment and diagnosis essential, and therefore new assessment instruments need to be developed for the major factors (such as level of individuation) that have to be assessed. The clinical picture of some psychological disorders are different from those known in the West, and therefore the criteria of normality and pathology need to be redetermined to fit the Arab/Muslim norms.

Chapter 4

Individuation Among Arabs/Muslims

The perception of childhood and adolescence as distinct periods in an individual's life is a modern one. In the ancient era there was no concept of childhood; many infants were treated harshly, and deformed or illegitimate babies were actually killed. Boys in Sparta in ancient Greece were exposed to a strict regime: As infants, they took cold-water baths, and at age 7 they were removed from their homes to live in army barracks where they were often beaten or deprived of food for days to instill in them the discipline of warriors (deMause, 1974). In the medieval ages children were considered family possessions and treated almost as miniature adults. Only in the seventeenth and eighteenth centuries did attitudes toward children and child rearing begin to change, and children started going to school (Shaffer, 1996).

Until the 1800s teenagers were considered capable of doing adult work and starting families. There was no defined period called adolescence, and young people did not go through the modern experience of adolescence, with its major emphasis on crystallizing personal identity. The "identity crisis" of adolescence was created only in the modern era, when people became concerned with identity issues (Monte & Sollod, 2003). Even today some of the world's cultures, such as that of the St. Lawrence Eskimos and some tribes in Africa, have no concept of adolescence as a distinct phase (Keith, 1985). These historical and cultural differences in the concepts of childhood and adolescence reflect a basic truth—that the stages of psychological development of the Western world, such as infancy, childhood, and adolescence with its "identity crisis," are far from universal, and but rather are, culture dependent. In 1996 Shaffer made this observation:

> No single portrait of development is accurate for all cultures, social classes, or racial and ethnic groups. . . . We should not automatically assume that developmental sequences observed in samples of North American or European children (the most heavily studied population) are optimal, or even that they characterize persons developing in other eras or cultural settings. . . . Only by adopting a cultural/historical perspective can we fully appreciate the richness and diversity of human development. (p. 8).

THE BIRTH OF THE INDIVIDUAL

The foundations of today's Western concepts of childhood and adolescence were laid about a hundred years ago by the work of Stanley Hall (1891, 1904) and Sigmund Freud (1900/1964a, 1940/1964b). The emergence of these concepts at this time was not by chance, but rather a result of the social, political, economic, and cultural development that had taken place in Europe and North America in the previous two centuries. Industrialization, capitalism, democracy, and the foundation of the national states created a climate that enabled the emergence of individualism in the West. Individualism brought a newborn into the world: the *individual,* an independent legitimate entity. This "being" had not been known before, and therefore nobody had been interested in learning about him. Only after the birth of the individual did a need arise to study and learn about his development. What are his characteristics and qualities? What are the factors that direct and control his behavior? These urgent questions led to the development of psychology as a science that intended to describe the development, personality, and psychopathology of the individual, and to learn how to control his behavior through education and psychotherapy. Psychology, therefore, was an inevitable by-product of the emergence of individualism in the West, and Western theories of psychology attempted to describe, as best they could, the independent modern individual. Since other societies in Asia, Africa, and South America are not individualistic, it is reasonable to question the universality of the basic psychological concepts that have been developed and applied in the West, and to be open to revise them according to a culturally sensitive perspective. New concepts and theories that are based on an *emic* understanding of cultures (i.e., from the perspective of a participant in the culture) need to be developed.

This chapter may help Western therapists and counselors to become aware of the unique characteristics of psychosocial development of Arab/Muslim children that are not typical to the Western developmental perspective. Mental health professionals may notice variations of these characteristics among some Arab/Muslim immigrants with whom they work. Understanding these characteristics properly within the cultural context may help professionals avoid misunderstandings, pathologizing, or culturally insensitive interventions.

BASIC CONCEPTS IN WESTERN THEORIES OF DEVELOPMENT

Two characteristics identify the Western theories of development. First, they are reductionist and unidimensional (Pedersen, 1999), and second, they describe a process of individuation that ends in an independent personality.

One-Factorial Theories of Development

One group of theories focuses on *cognitive* development. Hall (1891) started to explore the contents of children's minds and discovered that the "logic" of young children is not very logical at all. Piaget's theory also focused on the cognitive development of children and found "standard" stages of development among his sample population (Piaget, 1950, 1970). Freud moved the focus of development to *instincts*. For Freud the child's development is basically a development in sexual instincts. He also identified "standard" psychosexual stages of development in which the body zone and expression of the sexual instinct develop (Freud, 1940/1964b). Many post-Freudian theories (e.g., Erikson, 1950) emphasized the development in the *interpersonal* domain. Object-relation theories described in detail how the infant-mother relation develops, and identified "standard" stages of interpersonal development (Mahler, Bergman, & Pine, 1975). Along with the emergence of family system theories, the child's development came to be perceived as part of the family's development (Bigner, 1994). The one-factorial perspective produced some simplistic "either-or" dichotomic questions to which a lot of energy and large portions of publications were devoted: Is development instinctual or interpersonal? Is it a process of maturity or learning? Is it determined by heredity or environment? Is behavior determined in infancy (past) or adulthood (present)? Less dogmatic scholars asked these questions in a less definitive way: To what extent do the factors of instinctual versus interpersonal, maturity versus learning, heredity versus environment, or past versus present influence development? These questions are misleading because they miss the systemic perspective and deny that all these factors influence the child's development together, and they are all continuously and multi-directionally interacting (Dwairy, 1997c).

Reducing human development to the development of one factor is, in fact, part of the reductionism that prevails in the Western scientific perspective. In the last few centuries not only did the individual become distinct from the family, but the mind also became distinct from the body, and the body organs became distinct domains of research and expertise too. This atomism and reductionism fits the scientific zeitgeist that prevails in the West, but it is far from the holistic experience of people in collective societies, where individual and family as well as mind and body are inseparable entities (Dwairy, 1997a). It does not fit the holistic personality of Arabs, for whom the individual is an inseparable part of the family and for whom thoughts, emotions, values, and body are one undivided entity (see Chapter 5). These cultural differences challenge the one-dimensional "standard" stages of development and question their universality. All these theories, whether cognitive, instinctual, or interpersonal, are challenged when they are applied to Muslim infants (such as in Afghanistan and Pakistan) and Arab infants (such as in Sudan or south Egypt). In these societies mothers' milk is the major source of nutrition; breastfeeding does not terminate until the 2nd or 3rd year of life; and infants may be breastfed by another women in addition to or instead of the biological mother. Children are raised within extended families by a group of caregivers, and they do not attend nursery or kindergartens as most Western infants do. Of course, the child-parents relationship in these societies is different from that in the West, where infants grow within nuclear families and have different feeding and educational stages. Because of these differences all "standard" stages of development (such as oral, rapprochement, or preoperational) and sequences of development become questionable when applied to Arabs and Muslims.

Cultural Influences on Development

The influence of culture on emotional and social development is more obvious than on the cognitive development. Although Piaget admitted that cultural factors might influence cognitive development, he continued to describe the child as an isolated scientist, exploring the world and making critical discoveries largely on her own. Lev Vygotsky criticized Piaget's theory and offered a socio-cultural viewpoint of development. He thought that infants are born with a few "elementary mental functions," such as attention, perception, and memory, that are eventually transformed by the culture into "higher mental functions." Some cultures may foster abstract thinking and others may foster concrete observation (Vygotsky, 1934/1962; 1930/1978). Now it is known that reaching the *formal* abstract level of thinking is a matter of culture and that people belonging to a society in which formal schooling is nonexistent will not solve Piaget's formal-operational problems (Dasen, 1977; Dasen & Heron, 1981).

Vygotsky actually offered an alternative to the one-dimensional theory of Piaget. He claimed that cognitive development could not be understood in isolation from interpersonal development within a certain culture. Cross-cultural research on memory indicated interesting differences in memory strategies between people in Western industrialized societies and nonindustrialized societies, whose most important memory tasks might involve recalling locations and knowing one's orientation in a landscape. Australian aboriginal children, for example, are better than their Anglo-Australian peers at remembering locations in natural settings (Kearins, 1981), and African adolescents display a better recall of orally transmitted stories than do American adolescents (Dube, 1982). Arab Bedouins are known to have a superior ability to detect and interpret traces of any creature that has passed in their area, to forecast the weather according to environmental signs, and to compose herbal medicine. Western theories of development have not addressed the development of these abilities which are so vital for survival in the Arabian Desert.

In a comparison between the performance of Arab and Jewish students in Israel in the Wechsler intelligence test, Arab students were found to be better than Jews at memorizing information, while Jews were better at abstract thinking and reasoning. These differences were attributed to the differences in child rearing and socialization: Arab students are continually directed by authoritarian parents or teachers who leave limited space for personal thinking, judgment, and reasoning (Dwairy, 1998a).

These cultural differences fit the emphasis on memorizing in Islam. Muslims are required literally to memorize their holy book, the Qur'an. Memorizing in Islam is important in order to apply *qeyas* (knowing through mensuration or measurement), the Arab/Muslim epistemology according to which Muslims find directives to the truth (see Chapter 2). According to *qeyas*, the Muslim should solve a new problem by measuring it against a similar one that had been addressed or answered by the Prophet or in the Qur'an, and then apply the old solution to the new problem and behave accordingly. This rooted way of thinking among Arabs/Muslims does not, of course, foster personal judgment, reasoning, or creative thinking, but rather it encourages people to understand, memorize, and follow directives. Accordingly, in this context cognitive development is not likely to end in formal thinking as Piaget claimed. Western psychologists who administer intelligence tests to Arab/Muslim immigrants need to interpret the profile of the results according to these characteristics. Memorizing is expected to be better than abstract reasoning.

Theories of development that emphasize one factor, be it cognitive, instinctual, or interpersonal, in fact miss the sociocultural factors that were emphasized by Vygotsky and that are able to explain the cross-cultural differences in child development.

The Separation-Individuation Process

The ideological underpinnings of Western theories view the person as an individual and self-contained unit (Sampson, 1988). Accordingly, Western theories of development, especially those that focus on interpersonal development, emphasize an individuation process that ends in the creation of an independent identity. According to these theories, psychological development is a separation-individuation process. This process has been addressed by different psychologists using different terminology, but all are agreed that normal development starts in full dependency and ends in full independency.

Freud claimed that after the 5th year of life children already possess an almost independent structure of personality. The concept of transference implies that interpersonal behavior after age 5 is almost independent of the social environment, the child unconsciously repeating and transferring his or her early relationship with parents to the present interpersonal relationships. Freud claimed that after age 5, through a process of identification with the same-sex parent, the child possesses identity (Freud, 1900/1964a, 1940/1964b). According to Freud, the internal unconscious structure of personality determines and explains the behavior of children, adolescents, and adults.

Erikson (1950) emphasized the social factors in child development, but saw the formation of an independent ego-identity as a necessary stage in the normal development of children. He described the stages that lead to autonomous ego-identity: First, children gain basic trust (0–1 years), then seek autonomy (1–3 years) and move on toward initiation (3–6 years) and industry (6–12 years), until they achieve ego-identity in late adolescence. According to Erikson the formation of one's own sense of identity begins where the process of identification ends (Kroger, 1993).

Erikson actually described the ideal development in the Western society. According to that ideal the mentally healthy person is independent, autonomous, individuated, and internally controlled, takes responsibility for herself, and has an inner sense of self. A relationship is an understanding or contract freely undertaken by two autonomous individuals (Landrine, 1992; Sampson, 1988). Object-relation theories also focus on analyzing the process of separation-individuation in the first three years of life (Mahler, Bergman, & Pine, 1975) and its continuance into adolescence (Blos, 1967), until the individuation of the self is achieved.

According to Freud, Erikson, Mahler, or Blos, in an individualistic society dependency of adults may be considered as a disorder (e.g., dependent personality disorder) or a sort of fixation in, or transference from, early childhood relationships, because in such a society there is no justification for this dependency. In collective/authoritarian societies, on the other hand, where collective/authoritarian norms and values continue to be the major generator of behavior, assuming autonomy and independence is inappropriate. Adolescents and adults in such societies continue to be emotionally and socially dependent on their social environment (see Chapter 5).

Today, cross-cultural literature on the individuation of adolescents does not position autonomy opposite relatedness or connectedness. Individuated persons in the West also continue to be connected to their families, and therefore autonomy does not necessarily mean separateness or a lack of social caring. Kagitcibasi (1996) claims that autonomy and relatedness are two basic human needs, which, though apparently conflicting, are in fact compatible. She suggests that autonomy should be understood in two dimensions: *interpersonal distance*, which is the degree of distancing of self from others, and *autonomous functioning*, which is the degree to which a person is a self-governing agent and subject only to his own rule or values. According to Kagitcibasi, despite the fact that child-parent relationships in urbanized and industrialized portions of collective societies are moving toward greater independence, most of the people still display continuity in a close-knit interaction pattern. Therefore, it is typical in these societies to find a person to be both autonomous and still related to others.

Parenting Styles, Individuation, and Arab/Muslim Adolescents

In the last few decades empirical researchers have studied the socialization styles adopted in Arab homes and schools. Many studies found that an authoritarian or abusive socialization style is adopted toward Arab children (Achoui, 2003). In their study of Arab youth, Hatab and Makki (1978) found that the majority reported following their parents' direction in most of the important areas of their life: social behavior, interpersonal relationships, marriage, occupational preference, and political attitudes. Some reports indicated that physical and emotional abuse is a widespread style of parenting in Egypt (Saif El-Deen, 2001), Bahrain (Al-Mahroos, 2001), Kuwait (Qasem, Mustafa, Kazem, & Shah, 1998), Jordan (Al-Shqerat & Al-Masri, 2001) and Morocco (Al-Kittani, 2000), especially among lower-class, uneducated parents and in large or dysfunctional families.

Some studies reported that parents and teachers tend to justify physical punishment. When Palestinian parents were asked about their socialization means, the majority reported that they talk to and verbally direct their children. When they were asked about what they would do if the child continued to disobey their directives, 88.8% reported that they would use *all* means to control the child (Dwairy, 1998a). In another study conducted in Saudi Arabia, 78.1% of teachers and parents justified corporal punishment to control the children's behavior (Al-Dahash, 1996).

Contrary to reports on the effect of authoritarian parenting in the West, some studies indicate that Arab children and youth are satisfied with authoritarian parenting (Hatab & Makki, 1978) and do not complain of the abusive-aggressive behavior of teachers (Dwairy, 1998a, ch. 3). Some other studies indicated that authoritarianism is not associated with any detriment to the mental health of Arab youth (Dwairy, 2004d; Dwairy & Menshar, in press). It seems that authoritarian socialization has a meaning and effect different from that known in the West when it is applied within an authoritarian culture such as the Arab/Muslim. Within this culture children consider the application of punishment as the normal duty of parents and teachers. In a study among Saudi female college students, 67.5% of the sample reported that they were physically punished at various stages in their life. When their attitudes toward physical punishments were studied, it was found that 65.1% of the students justified it (Achoui, 2003). Similar or worse results may be obtained in the general Saudi populace. However, Saudi society is considered among the stricter societies compared to other Arab/Muslim societies.

The acceptance of authority by Arab/Muslim adolescents and adults is, in fact, remote from the conflicts typically taking place in adolescence in the West. Timimi (1995) postulated that Arab youth do not experience identity crises in adolescence or achieve individual autonomy because their identity is enmeshed in that of the family, to which they are always loyal. Furthermore, Racy (1970) noted that in Arab countries adolescence is early, brief, and less stormy than in the West, with roles and opportunities being defined from birth. Female adolescents are expected to be modest and assume a role in the household duties, and male adolescents are expected to take part in the sustenance of the family. The range of individual identity is limited. Arab adolescents are not expected to act out, become self-centered, or engage in nonconformist behavior.

Despite the strict socialization used in the upbringing of female Arab/ Muslim children and adolescents, some studies indicate that authoritarian parenting and corporal punishment are actually applied more to boys than girls (Al-Shqerat & Al-Masri, 2001; Al-Kittani, 2000; Dwairy, 2004d). It seems that boys dare more to challenge the authority of the Arab/Muslim family, while girls tend to submit to their families, thereby avoiding punishment.

With regard to individuation and independence, authoritarian socialization is assumed to generate a dependent identity and a less individuated self. Indeed, when the ego identity of Palestinian Arab adolescents was tested by an "objective measure of ego-identity status" (OMEIS) of Adams, Shea, and Fitch (1979), it was found to be more "foreclosed" and "diffused" than that of the American youth (see Table 4.1). *Foreclosed* adolescents do not experience a crisis period, but rather adopt commitments from others (usually parents) and accept them as their own without shaping, modifying, or testing them for personal fit. *Diffused* adolescents do not experience a need or desire to explore alternatives and/or deal with questions of their identity. The identity of male adolescents was more foreclosed than that of the females (Dwairy, 2004b). The interconnectedness with their parents as tested by a "multigenerational interconnectedness scale" (MIS) of Gavazzi and Sabatelli (1987, 1988) was of a higher level than that found among Western sample populations. The Palestinian Arab adolescents displayed a higher level of emotional, financial, and functional interdependence with their parents. Female adolescents displayed a higher level of financial dependence on their parents than males did (Dwairy, 2004b). Among the Arabs/ Muslims in Israel, the ego identity of Bedouin adolescents was the most foreclosed by their parents.

These results concerning parenting styles, individuation, and mental health are most relevant to rural Arab societies. There are some indications that this style of child-parent relationship has changed among urbanized and educated families, or among immigrant Arab/Muslim families in the West. In a comparison of Egyptian rural and urban adolescents, female urban adolescents reported experiencing a more authoritarian parenting style than did either boys or their counterpart rural female adolescents. They displayed a higher level of behavior

Table 4.1. Means and standard deviation of Palestinian Arab (N = 518) and American adolescents in OMIES (N = >2000) and MIS (N = 335)

Scale	Subscale	Statistic	Arabs	Americans	T	P<
OMEIS*	Foreclosed	M	19.14	16.25	7.09	.0001
		SD	5.35	5.22		
	Diffused	M	19.89	15.60	4.66	.0001
		SD	5.27	3.29		
MIS**	Emotional	M	4.5	3.8	5.90	.0001
		SD	.79	.91		
	Financial	M	5.4	4.2	6.38	.0001
		SD	1.23	.96		
	Functional	M	4.6	4.3	1.62	.05
		SD	.99	1.29		
	Total MIS	M	14.6	12.4	5.99	.0001
		SD	2.47	2.57		

* American results are based on Bennion and Adams (1986).
** American results are based on Gavazzi and Sabatelli (1988).

problems and spent more time under the observation and control of their parents (Dwairy & Menshar, in press). Immigrant families in the West enforce stricter control of their children, especially daughters, than they did in their homeland (see Chapter 3). It seems that the security that tradition usually provides in rural areas in Arab/Muslim countries is challenged in urban areas or in the West, where adolescents are exposed to modern and liberal values, and thus new conflicts within the family are created that push the parents toward being more controlling and stricter in relation to their daughters.

As mentioned, many studies have found that authoritarian parenting is not associated with the harm to good mental health assumed by Western researchers. One interesting study, among Arab gifted and nongifted children, though it did indicate a significant correlation between authoritative parenting and mental health among both groups, found that for the gifted group, authoritarian parenting was associated less with good mental health. Among the gifted children, authoritarian parenting was associated with low self-esteem and higher identity, anxiety, phobia, depression, and conduct disorders (Dwairy, 2004e).

These normative psychocultural characteristics may be misunderstood or pathologized by counselors and psychotherapists who adopt the Western perspective of development. Fisek and Kagitcibasi (1999) have commented that in the Turkish family authoritarianism should not be considered as oppression, emotional connectedness as enmeshment or fusion, or the collective familial-self as constriction or developmental arrest. Western counselors and therapists who work with Arab/Muslim families should not consider psychosocial dependency as a fixation, immaturity, or transference from early childhood, but rather as an appropriate and functional behavior that is based on correct reality testing and understanding of the controlling social reality in collective cultures.

Western mental health professionals are encouraged not only to understand the core dynamics of the Arab/Muslim immigrant family but also to avoid stereotypic understanding and to be aware of the diversity within these families. While counselors and therapists bear in mind these core dynamics, they may continue to be open to understanding the dynamics within a specific family in therapy and to listening to the client and the family in order to understand their values, norms, and concerns. Once they have discovered an authoritarian parenting style or interdependency between a client and her family, they should not jump to conclusions and work toward achieving more independence for the family's member or try to enforce the law to put a stop to the authoritarian parenting. Rather, counselors are recommended to look for change within the collective cultural system of the client. More concrete directives to counselors and therapists will be presented in Chapters 9 and 10.

SUMMARY

Within a collective sociocultural system children are raised to maintain cohesion, harmony, and connectedness. Authoritarian socialization in homes and schools is very common and normative. As a result, adolescence is not expected to be a stormy period in traditional Arab/Muslim societies and does not conclude in the building of an independent ego identity. Authoritative socialization, in fact, seems to contribute to the mental health of Arab/Muslim adolescents; nevertheless, and unlike in the West, authoritarianism seems not to be detrimental to the mental health of the Arab/Muslim youth.

Chapter 5

Collective Personality of Arabs/Muslims

If the Arab/Muslim adult does not have an independent personality, but rather has a personality that is enmeshed in the collective identity, can Western personality theories be useful in understanding the Arab/Muslim personality and behavior? Can these individualistic theories mislead a therapist's understanding and then his intervention? Are different personality constructs or concepts needed to understand the collective personality of Arabs/Muslims?

PERSONALITY THEORIES

As stated in the previous chapter, the concept of the personality is a comparatively new one that emerged 200 years ago. It appeared together with the emergence of individualism in Europe, because only then did seeking to understand the individual become necessary. Before the era of individualism the individual was not a distinct entity, and roles rather than personality were the elements that constituted the person (Sampson, 1989). After the birth of the "individual" and the ensuing social recognition that she is an independent entity with her own needs, rights, attitudes, and values, personality theories appeared to explain this "newborn" (Dwairy, 2002a).

Theories of personality typically intend to describe, explain, predict, and control the individual's behavior. They consider the personality to be a relatively stable entity across situations and to have originated "within" the individual (Ewen, 2003). Most of these theories try to explain the behavior of the individual in intrapsychic terms, each theory providing sets of hypothetical intrapsychic constructs and processes. Among these constructs are the id, ego, superego, unconscious, self, false self, ideal self, inner thoughts, and traits. Among the intrapsychic processes are conflicts, dissonance, homeostasis, repression, and other defense mechanisms (Dwairy, 2002a). Accordingly, depression, anxiety, or aggression may be explained in terms of unconscious processes (psychoanalytic), self (humanistic), inner thoughts (cognitive), or traits (trait theories).

All Western personality theories posit that intrapsychic constructs initially develop from the past experiences of the individual with her social environment, but are internalized at a later stage to direct behavior, and become almost independent of the social environment. Consequently, consistency of behavior across situation and time is expected, because social influences work on behavior only through the representation of internal constructs already formulated during the course of development. Hence, the effect these theories attribute to social environment is almost completely limited to the past (childhood), whereas in the present the personality becomes a major factor that buffers social influences and guides behavior. Only behavioral theories give priority to current social factors in terms of stimuli and reinforcements that determine and control behavior. Western psychologists who adopt this individualistic perspective of personality may be confused when they try to understand the personality of an Arab/Muslim immigrant. They may find confusion between the internal constructs of the client and her family's norms and values. They will find it difficult, or sometimes impossible, to differentiate between the individual's personality and that of the family. Metaphorically speaking, an encounter with a traditional Arab/Muslim individual is an encounter with a group of people that live inside her and still play a major role in directing her behavior. The collective personality of Arabs/Muslims will be exemplified by a case later in this chapter.

Firas: A Case of Intrafamial Conflict

Firas is a 32-year-old Arab/Muslim bachelor who suffers from headaches and difficulty in breathing. He is overwhelmingly immersed in obsessive thoughts concerning the precision of his daily actions and his memory. He is concerned whether he walks, eats, drives, or writes accurately, whether he closed the door before he left the house, and whether he will remember to make the payments to the bank in time.

Three years ago he fell in love with a girl in the village. His father rejected her as a wife for his son because she was a member of the opposing family in the local council elections. He tried to argue with his father but found all his brothers and the whole family stood with the father. He came to feel that he was an egoist and that he was disregarding the family interest and convenience. He therefore felt ashamed, retreated from girls, and stopped considering marriage. He said that he loves his family very much and that for him relinquishing the girl was easier than hurting his family.

Firas works in a factory that belongs to his family and spends most of his income on financing the college expenses of his two younger brothers, as compensation for not being able to go to college himself after he successfully finished high school. "I do this because I love them; if they earn a higher education, it is as if I had learned," he said. The rest of his income goes to the shared family budget for the building of five apartments for the five male sons.

Two years ago the conflict with his family's opponents was resumed. The two families engaged in a fight during which his father was attacked and injured. "When I saw my father fallen and bleeding, I felt deep hurt. My father is second after God," he said. The day after the fight he went to where the opponent family lived and burned a car that belonged to them. He said, "I did that to restore and save the face of my father and my family." He expected his family to appreciate his attitude and his actions. Instead, his family resented his reactions because they wanted to give a chance to a third respected family, which had intervened to achieve reconciliation between the two families. As a response to his "favor" Firas expected the family to share the expenses of replacing the car he burnt, but when he asked them to contribute, they refused and called him impulsive, reckless, and irresponsible. He argued with them and expressed some anger and rage. He complained to his mother about the "betrayal" of the family. She expressed sympathy mixed with helplessness and made him understand that he should avoid annoying his suffering father who was still in the hospital. When he reported this event in therapy he did not express direct anger or rage, but instead said "God, forgive them," and cited the Qur'an and said *"La taqul lahom off"* [Don't express disgust toward them (parents).]

Last year Firas's younger brother and sister married another brother and sister in marriages arranged between the two families. Despite feeling that his family was neglecting him, he shared actively in the marriages and publicly displayed happiness and joy. When he was asked about his feelings in therapy, he was able to express anger and rage toward his family but immediately said, "but I was happy for them. They are, after all, my family. They did the right thing for the family." When he was asked about the way he expresses his anger, he asserted, "I can't express that to my family." The only people with whom he was able to talk openly about his rage were his two cousins, who had experienced similar rejection in their own family: "When we meet we do not curb our tongues when we describe our fathers and families." Firas reported that he meets these cousins frequently and when he is with them he feels free from his obsessive thoughts and physical symptoms.

Is the main "drama" in Firas's life taking place in the intrapsychic "arena" or in the intrafamilial one? To what extent does Firas have autonomous ego, self, and superego? To what extent are his needs differentiated from the needs and interests of the family? To what extent does the familial pressure "refuel" and activate his ego and superego day by day to make him submit to the family will? Is his avoidance of expressing anger caused by unconscious defense mechanisms (repression or denial) or by a conscious coping technique to avoid external pressure or rejection? If an unconscious intrapsychic process is causing the obsessive thoughts and the physical symptoms, how can one explain the immediate relief he feels when he ventilates his anger with his cousins? Within the interdependence of Firas's social-economic system, is he capable of being independent? Is it wise or possible to help him think, "I can express my anger to the family," instead of his current thinking, "I can't express my anger to my family?" Is it wise or possible to help him develop an independent self and fulfill his needs and express his feelings regardless of his family's expectations? These issues will be addressed in the following sections.

PERSONALITY AND CULTURE

Theorists over the past few decades have begun to question the universality of Western personality theories and have been examining the role culture plays in the development of personality. The *Journal of Cross-Cultural Psychology and Research* published a special issue (1998, Vol. 29, No. 1), "Personality and Its Measurement in a Cross-Cultural Perspective." Markus and Kitayama (1998) claimed in this issue that Western theories viewed the personality as an indigenous, bounded, coherent, stable, autonomous, and free system that may work well in individualistic societies, but has little relevance in other, collective societies.

The study of culture and its impact on personality is only at its beginning. Paul Pedersen (1990) was the first to consider the multicultural perspective as the fourth force in psychology, after psychoanalysis, humanism, and the behavioral-cognitive approach. Taking Pedersen's idea one step further, one can then postulate that among people who live in a collective cultural system, the collective social net may be considered as much more than a fourth factor. It is a metafactor that influences and shapes the other three forces. Social norms and values of the collective, in fact, determine the dynamics of the id, ego, and superego, defense mechanisms, and guilt that are supposed to explain behavior according to psychoanalysis, and determine the self, ideal self, and self-fulfillment that, according to humanistic approaches, are the basic constructs of personality. The collective social net also exerts an almost direct influence on environmental contingencies as well as on the client's inner thoughts or axioms, which are emphasized in behavioral-cognitive theories. Accordingly, Arab/Muslim norms and values that operate through the family determine the intrapsychic constructs of personality. These constructs are collective and unindividuated. The boundaries between the individual's personality and the collective social net are open and fragile, the social net being the powerful and dominant side that activates the personality constructs. Consequently, behavior and personality within collective societies could be better explained by external cultural factors (norms, values, roles, and familial authority) than by intrapsychic structures and processes that have not been individuated.

A review of the cross-cultural literature on personality (Dwairy, 1998a,

2002a; Markus & Kitayama, 1998; Singelis, 1994; Triandis, 1995) reveals the following characteristics of collective peoples:

1. The self is not autonomous, but is connected to an extended family or tribe. It directs its energy toward achieving group, rather than personal, goals.
2. The behavior of the individual is more situational and contextual than dispositional. It is controlled by external factors such as roles and norms rather than internal factors such as personal attribution of behavior.
3. Priority is given to interpersonal responsibilities rather than to justice and individual rights.
4. More other-focused emotions (e.g., sympathy and shame) are experienced than ego-focused ones.

These differences in needs, emotions, values, and social behavior are profound and actually cover almost the whole area of personality, and as such, should be construed as much more than a trait of personality. Such comprehensive differences call for a dynamic explanation of personality that acknowledges the major roles of family, society, and culture. However, theories of personality continue to lack a psychosocial dynamic personality theory that defines constructs and processes that explain and predict the behavior of people who possess a collective, unindividuated personality.

THE COLLECTIVE PERSONALITY OF ARABS/MUSLIMS

In order to understand and predict the behavior of people who live in collective social systems, one should not detach personality (intrapsychic) factors from social-cultural ones, but rather the concept of personality should be modified and expanded to encompass a social layer that works in conjunction with internal constructs and processes. Personality in these societies is a collective construct that describes the interpersonal dynamics between the individual and her family or tribe. It includes social factors (norms, values, roles, and authority), on the one hand, and intrapsychic factors, on the other. It should be noted here, however, that intrapsychic factors are typically not independent of external factors in these societies, but rather are dominated by them (Dwairy, 2002a).

Taking the Turkish case as an example of the Muslim world, Fisek and Kagitcibasi (1999) asserted that the Turkish culture is located at the authoritarian-relatedness (or collective) end of the continuum, while the prototypic Western culture falls closer to the horizontal-separateness (or liberal-individualistic) end. These cultural differences impact the meaning of the *self*. Unlike the Western self, the prototypic Turkish self is not an individualized and autonomous one, but is familial and connected. Reliance on emotional interconnectedness within the Turkish family remains a central feature of one's experience.

The Arab/Muslim family is an economic social unit in which its members find economic as well as emotional and social support. Individuals cannot easily achieve independence because, in order to attempt differentiation and independence, the individual must find means to survive by his own resources. When the state does not provide the basic needs of its citizens (as described in Chapter 4), independence of the family seems almost impossible. This economic dependency on the family leads to psychological dependency.

Intrafamilial Rather Than Intrapsychic Conflict

Within this interdependent system, the main conflict that the individual experiences is with the social norms, values, and expectations. These external pressures are the main source of control because opposing them means losing vital familial support. The internal constructs of control such as ego, self, or superego are therefore not autonomous. They continue to be directed by external pressures in adulthood.

The main drama of Arabs/Muslims' life takes place within the intrafamilial domain rather than the intrapsychic one. As we saw in the case of Firas, the main conflict was between his needs and the expectations and pressures of his family. His ego and superego were "refueled" and activated by the response of the family, and his ideal self was redefined by them day by day. Once he allowed himself to act out his needs and feelings he was faced with a familial repressing response that threatened him. After each such encounter he felt threatened and ashamed. He was not able to express his authentic feelings to his family or others in his immediate social environment, but was able to do so in his meeting with the two cousins.

The conflict between Firas's needs and his own superego was minor. He did not feel anxiety or guilt because of his anger at the family. His anger was hidden or separate, not from his own consciousness—he was able to express his anger to his cousins—but from his family and friends. Firas was avoiding any public expression of anger because he was consciously avoiding the familial social sanctions, not because of unconscious repression or denial.

The Family as the Source of Threat, Esteem, and Joy

The Arab/Muslim family is the source of threat as well as the source of joy and happiness. The response of the family may foster shame feelings when the individual displays any deviance from the family consensus, and may bring satisfaction and happiness when the individual's deeds and attitudes fit the will of the family and add credit to the family reputation and coherence. Personal accomplishments do not count if the family does not approve them. For instance, if an adolescent manifested an artistic talent that was not approved by the family, he could not be proud and enjoy any accomplishment in arts. The kind of happiness that comes from outside is much different from the happiness that comes from self-fulfillment, which may be the commonly known happiness in the West. Firas was ready to do anything—relinquishing his love, burning the car of the opponent's family, displaying happiness at the weddings of his brother and sister—in order to avoid rejection and gain the approval of the family.

When the self is not differentiated from the family's identity, self-concept and self-esteem will have collective meanings, dependent on the family's reputation and approval and reflections of the family's identity. Notice that Firas's obsessive thoughts are almost a literal translation of what his family said about his behavior. They described him as impulsive, reckless, and irresponsible, and as a result he began seeing himself accordingly, and was not sure that he had done the right things. The opinion of his family was so powerful and effective that it made him lose his basic trust in being able to walk, eat, drive, or write correctly.

Social Mechanisms Rather Than Unconscious Defense Mechanisms

Because the main source of suppression is external rather than internal, Arabs/ Muslims need social mechanisms to manipulate the external oppressor rather than unconscious defense mechanisms that are intended to manipulate the superego. Three main social mechanisms help the Arab/Muslim individual cope with the intrafamilial conflict: *mosayara, istighaba,* and identification with the oppressor (Dwairy, 2002a; Noor El-Deen, 2000).

Mosayara (getting along) is a central value that directs the individual to hide real feelings and attitudes and to display reactions that meet the expectations of others. It helps to maintain the coherence of the collective at the expense of the expression of personal feelings and attitudes. *Istighaba* is the other side of the coin, according to which individuals find ways to express their authentic feelings and attitudes in the absence (*ghiab*) of familial or social observation. For instance, within a close and safe group they may express opposite attitudes to those expressed in public, or they may behave indecently. *Istighaba* to *mosayara* is like the valve of a pressure cooker. In a study conducted in Lebanon and Bahrain (UNDP, 2003, ch. 3), which examined how adolescent Arab girls cope with their parents' authority, it was found that girls use lies and behave badly away from social control, on the one hand, but in public adhere to their parents and exhibit conformity to social rules, on the other.

These two social coping mechanisms are complementary, one accomplishes what the other does not. The two mechanisms together achieve an impossible mission: The *istighaba* enables ventilation of emotions that the *mosayara* prohibits, and the *mosayara* maintains the social approval that the content of *istighaba* would impair if it were expressed publicly. Notice that these mechanisms accomplish this mission by virtue of social manipulations and lies. When others are the source of the control and threat, one needs to manipulate them, just as one needs to manipulate the superego when it is the source of the control. However, Westerners use unconscious defense mechanisms to manipulate the superego, whereas Arabs/Muslims are well aware of the contents that are expressed in *istighaba* although the wider social environment is not. Figure 5.1 gives a graphic representation of how coping mechanisms work in the collective and individuated personalities.

Often *istighaba* works in coordination with *mosayara*. The individual meets people and expresses authentic feelings toward others (*istighaba*). Frequently the others do not agree with these feelings and needs, but employ *mosayara* and listen, while hiding their authentic attitudes, and even express some identification with the expressed attitudes.

In the case of Firas we noticed how he employed *mosayara* and *istighaba* to survive within the family that conditions its approval and support on submission. He tried in every way that he could to get along with his family and displayed the emotions that pleased them. He obeyed and stood beside them in their fight with the other family as well as in the marriages of his sister and brother, despite his anger. He spent his money to help his brothers. On the other hand, he found a safe place with his cousins to ventilate his oppressed feelings.

Identification with the oppressor mechanism was mentioned by Freire (1970/1995, 1992/1994) to describe how the victims of the social and political oppression in Brazil identified with the oppressor to survive the oppression. Identification with the oppressor is another psychosocial mechanism that helps Arabs/Muslims survive within the interdependent system. They identify with the family even when it is oppressive, and actually justify the familial oppression. One of the extreme manifestations of this psychosocial mechanism is the self-blame of battered and abused women. Among Malaysian Muslims, for instance, most abused wives blame themselves and remain in their marriage (Yusooff, 2003). One can assume that they deny their anger; however, this kind of denial is not purely intrapsychic, but rather is mobilized by an intensive external social blame that threatens the women.

As mentioned in Chapter 1, Arab citizens in Israel rely on their families rather than on the state when seeking work or building a house. Firas was therefore economically dependent on his family. He worked in a factory that belongs to the family. The family took care of building houses for all its sons. The identity of Firas and the family's identity are almost one identity. Firas identified with his oppressing father and family. He felt personally hurt when his

Figure 5.1. Collective Personality Versus Individuated Personality

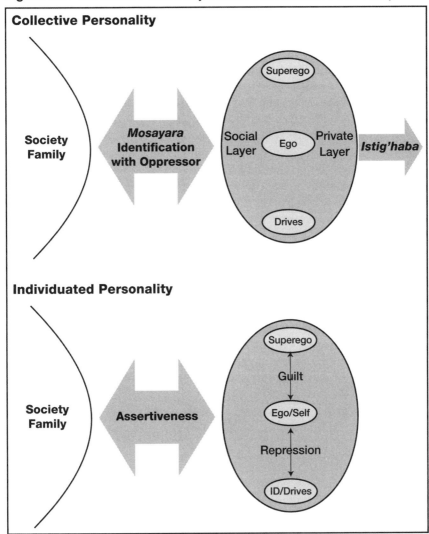

father was hurt. He financed the college education of his two brothers and felt as if he were fulfilling his own personal dream to learn in college. The reputation of the family was important to him. When he felt that this reputation was threatened, he was ready to do anything "to restore and save the face of my father and my family." When talking about the betrayal of his family, he said, "They are after all my family. They did the right thing for the family . . . God, forgive them." When his needs contradicted the will of the family, he was ready to sacrifice his needs and said, "For me, relinquishing the girl I loved is easier than hurting my family."

If one adopts the Western premise that everyone has an independent self, one may assume that identification with the oppressor includes denial and is a less conscious mechanism than are *mosayara* and *istighaba*. In fact, traditional Arabs/Muslims simply believe that they and their families are one entity. They are not aware of a personal self or identity that is differentiated from the family, and do not feel they are missing any part of their personality when they identify with their oppressive family.

Social Versus Private Layer of Personality

The lack of differentiation among Arabs/Muslims is not limited to the boundaries between the individual and the family, but exists within the individual too. The internal world of Arabs/Muslims tends to be fused, with no distinct differentiation between internal constructs, such as thoughts, emotions, attitudes, and values. In Chapter 1 I showed that the Arab/Muslim mind is a moral mind, and that thinking and reason are related to morals and intertwined with values (Al-Jabiri, 1991b, 2002). When the values are mixed up with reason, and the personal needs with the family's needs, the boundaries between the internal personality structures (id, self, ego, or superego) are blurred, and these constructs remain indistinct. When Firas was asked specifically about his feelings, thoughts, or values, he gave answers that fuse all these functions together without differentiating his and his family's feelings, thoughts, and values. To understand the Arab/Muslim, one needs to avoid reductionism and apply holistic and systemic thinking. Because Western theories of personality tend to be reductionist, employing limited distinct intrapsychic constructs to understand the person (Monte & Sollod, 2003), they are mostly inapplicable to the Arab/Muslim, for whom individuals are not distinct from the collective.

The main distinction that can be found within the indistinct (or fused) Arab/ Muslim' inner world is between the "social layer" and "private layer" of personality (Dwairy, 2002a; see also Fig. 5.1 above). The social layer includes all functions that serve the interests and coherence of the collective. It employs *mosayara* and identification with the oppressor to provide this service for the coherence of the collective. It includes all mental functions of memorizing, *qeyas* (finding solutions based on Qur'an and Sunna), and submission to the social norms and values. It enables the individual to see things through the eyes of the collective and judge them by its values. It is a mix of social ego and superego and includes mental abilities as well social values and morals.

The private layer of the Arab/Muslim personality fulfills the mission of ventilating the socially forbidden needs or expressions at a distance from social and familial censorship. It serves the authentic personal needs and feelings by employing the *istighaba*. This layer allows the individual to restore his esteem, and avoid the position of being a robot that fulfills others' orders. In Laing's terms (1959), the private layer may be seen as protecting the Arab/Muslim individual from ontological anxieties such as engulfment, implosion, and petrification. The private layer, too, includes mental and social skills as well as values. To apply *istighaba* one must know how to choose the right content (of the talk or action) at the right context (people, place, and timing) to ventilate the forbidden feelings and needs. For instance, sexual feelings or negative feelings toward parents could not be ventilated in the nuclear family. Within the private layers some values are also at work. Secrets and keeping the content of the talk or action away from the relevant authority is one major value that people adhere to when they share in *istighaba* talk or action. Displaying sympathy and support to the one who ventilates his feelings is another situation where *mosayara* is applied.

In the encounter between him and his family, Firas followed the norms and employed *mosayara*. When he employed *istighaba* with his cousins, as well as when he allowed himself to express his anger in therapy, he was not detached from norms and values; he asked for the forgiveness of his family and was directed by the Islamic values through the *qeyas* to say that one should not express disgust toward one's parents. Note that using *mosayara* and *istighaba* is a zero-sum game. When Firas employs *istighaba* his symptoms disappear. Similarly, the *istighaba* and the expression of values within it is a zero-sum game. When in therapy Firas asked for forgiveness for his parents and cited the Qur'an, he felt no guilt despite the expression of anger toward his parents.

Consistency and Individual Differences

The content that is expressed by the two layers of personality is frequently inconsistent. One may express positive feelings and attitudes in *mosayara* and express opposite feelings and attitudes in *istighaba*. The behavior as well as the expressed feelings and attitudes are contextual. The consistency exists within each layer, but not between layers, of personality. The social behavior is usually predictable because it follows the expectations of the collective. Conversely, people's private expressions are frequently unpredictable. When disclosed, they may astonish the people who have known the person in public. Typically, this disclosure is followed by social and familial sanctions.

Firas's behavior was obviously inconsistent. He expressed love and respect to his family in one context, and displayed rage and used bad language when he was with his cousins. The people who see Firas in the family and public context observe a consistently loyal son. The cousins observe consistency in Firas too: He is always dissatisfied and angry with his family.

Individual differences in the public social life of Arabs/Muslims are minor and can be attributed to two factors: level of individuation and social status. The level of individuation determines the proportion of the personality that is taken up by the social layer. The social layer of a less individuated person is typically dominant (or prevailing), and therefore the deviations from the expected social behavior and the individual differences are minor. More individuated people allow themselves more freedom of self-expression. The other factor that generates individual differences is social status. This factor is related to the familial affiliation, gender, age, and profession of the individual. Accordingly, the social behavior of rich and educated people will differ from that of poor and uneducated ones. Women's behavior differs from men's, and old peoples' behavior differs from that of the young. Generally speaking, educated, rich, male, and older people tend to conform less to traditions. In addition, the social behavior depends much on one's profession. A teacher, for instance, is expected to be a role model and behave differently from a driver or farmer.

The two factors mentioned above—level of individuation and social status—explain the individual differences much better than do the internal personality constructs suggested by the Western theories of personality. Accordingly, knowing the culture and status of Firas's family, and knowing his gender, age, and profession allows one to predict much of his behavior that would not have been predictable according to his internal personality constructs and processes alone. The diagnostic issue of personality will be discussed in Chapter 6.

PSYCHOPATHOLOGY

Psychopathology according to the Western perspective is a disorder in the intrapsychic domain. This perspective is based on the reductionistic distinction between individual and family and between mind and body (Dwairy, 2002a). According to the psychosocial dynamic system of the Arab/Muslim personality, these distinctions do not hold; individual and family, as well as mind and body are one integral system. Accordingly, the disorder is expected to be manifest indistinctly in any aspect of the whole system: interpersonal, intrapsychic, and somatic.

Normally the psychosocial system is balanced in terms of give and take; the familial support that the individual takes and the adherence that the individual gives. The private layer balances the social layers. This system is expected to achieve two things: maintain the cohesion of the family, and provide the individual with familial support. When one of these two objectives is not achieved a psychosocial-somatic deviation may be observed. (This topic will be discussed in detail in Chapter 7).

In the case of Firas, it was obvious that the *mosayara* he employed was not balanced with the support he received; in the end he did not gain the family approval. The intensive and comprehensive rejection of his attitudes and deeds made him lose his basic trust, and he started to worry about his ability to function. The ventilation he achieved by *istighaba* was not sufficient to balance the system; therefore he suffered from obsessive and somatic symptoms.

PSYCHOTHERAPY

Western psychotherapy typically aims to restore the intrapsychic order through "making what is unconscious conscious" and encouraging the individual to actualize the self and be "himself" or "herself." In the Arab/Muslim case this psychotherapy frequently generates tough confrontation between the individual and his or her family. When the individual is economically, socially, and psychologically dependent, one can expect that the individual will be the losing party in this confrontation, and one should therefore anticipate exacerbation of the problems. For Arab/Muslim people, psychotherapy should aim to find new order within the psychosocial-somatic system. Joining the family authority, revising the efficiency of the client's social coping mechanisms, and implementing indirect metaphoric interventions are basic directives for working with Arab/Muslim clients (see Chapters 9 and 11).

As for Firas, the therapist did not try to make him independent and did not encourage him to express his anger toward his family. Joining the father and employing his care to the family, helping Firas to revise the efficiency of the *mosayara* and find a better balance in his psychosocial system, and helping him to reorganize his world by metaphoric indirect ways (see Chapters 8 and 11) were the major components of therapy that helped him. Firas was directed to find Qur'anic verses that would help him revise his blind dependence on the family attitudes and enable him to rely on his own judgment. He was astonished when he realized that his obsessive thoughts were actually a literal translation of his family's description of his behavior. Cognitive-behavioral therapy helped him revise these descriptions and control his obsessive thoughts.

To understand the Arab/Muslim client, Western counselors and therapists should attempt to comprehend the whole psychosocial system and not limit themselves to psychodiagnosis of the client's inner world. Therefore, diagnostic tools should be used to assess the level of individuation, cultural beliefs, intrafamilial conflicts, and the efficiency of the social coping mechanisms of the client. The next chapter will analyze the diagnostic approach to the collective personality.

SUMMARY

The personality of Arabs/Muslims is a collective construct that includes social factors (e.g., norms) and intrapsychic factors. The family is the source of threat as well as the source of joy and happiness. The main conflict of Arabs/Muslims takes place within the intrafamilial domain rather than the intrapsychic one. Therefore, they need social mechanisms to manipulate the external pressure rather than unconscious defense mechanisms. These substantial differences in personality influence the conceptualization of psychological disorders and psychotherapy.

Chapter 6

Assessment Issues Among Arabs/Muslims

Assessment tools usually stem from a personality theory, which posits certain constructs and processes that should be evaluated in order to understand a person's behavior. Psychodynamic theory has led to the assessment of unconscious conflicts and defense mechanisms through projective techniques; humanistic theory, to assessment of self-concept and self-esteem; and behavioral theory, to the observation of behavior. Because the Arab/Muslim personality is qualitatively different from the individualistic one, issues of diagnosis should be radically revised according to an understanding of this population. Three main questions are addressed in this chapter:

1. Does the psychological construct or concept being measured have equivalent meanings among Arab/Muslims?
2. What are the main constructs that should be targeted in assessment?
3. How can counselors and clinicians adapt their assessment tools to Arab/Muslim clients?

CULTURE-BOUND MEANING OF TRAITS

Some clinical pictures are called *culture-bound syndromes* (Simon & Hughes, 1993). I would borrow that term to describe some traits and personality constructs. Some core constructs, such as *intelligence* and *independence*, are culture-bound; that is, they have substantially different meanings in relation to Westerners and to Arab/Muslims. When this is the case, the construct validity of a test is violated, and therefore counselors cannot compare cultures according to these constructs.

Intelligence and Social Competency

Lonner (1990) explained the different meanings of *intelligence*. In the West, one is intelligent if one is both smart and quick thinking, while in other cultures such as in Uganda, intelligence is associated with wisdom, slow thoughtfulness, and saying the appropriate thing. Similarly, Al-Jabiri (2002) explained the unique meaning of *'aql* in Arabic, which is translated as mind or reason, but, in fact, means "control" and has nothing to do with the Western meaning of reasoning or mind. Children are directed from early childhood to use their *'aql* when they misbehave or lose control. A person who is an *'aaqel* is one who is able to control herself and behave according to social expectations and values. Therefore, Al-Jabiri, who wrote several books concerning the Arabic *'aql*, claims that the mind in Islam is associated with morals and values much more than with logic and reasoning.

When Arab/Muslim children are raised in an authoritarian climate, they learn how to listen, memorize, obey the rules, and behave as expected, at the expense, of course, of experiencing trials and errors and developing free thinking and creativity. Compared to the performance of Jewish students in Israel on the WISC-R test, Arab students performed higher in the "information" and lower in the "comprehension" subtest (Dwairy, 1998a). These results indicate that Arab students learn to memorize and store information, but have difficulty understanding and judging a situation independently and then making their own decisions accordingly.

Since Arab/Muslims are used to adapting themselves to the Arab/Muslim social cultural system, their social competencies and social confidences are challenged once they move to live in the West. Within this new context they lose their "social compass" and may react either in an immature, dependent way or overreact in an aggressive way as a result of an unbearable frustration or threat. Counselors who work with Arab/Muslim immigrants need to know the social competency of these clients in two contexts: in the Arab/Muslim culture and in the new Western culture. The discrepancy in terms of a client's social functioning in the two cultures is expected to be large and has significant meaning. To exemplify this issue, consider for a moment an extreme example of a traditional Arab Bedouin person. An intelligent Bedouin knows exactly the Bedouin norms that direct him how to behave in every single social situation; he knows how to forecast the weather from the sky's color, the shape of the clouds, and other natural signals, how to orient himself in the monotonous desert environment, how to interpret the traces of travelers in that physical environment, and how to use desert herbal remedies. When this Bedouin moves to live in a modern Western society, he may be confused in many social settings, may not understand the weather TV forecast, may be disoriented on the highways, and may misuse or abuse the medical system and chemical medications.

Counselors should not be satisfied with knowing a client's disability in terms of the Western system, but should also know how the client has functioned in the homeland system. A low level of functioning in the Western system only is one thing, while a low level in both systems is quite another. The first case may be considered a common phenomenon among new immigrants who face typical social disorientation, and counselors may need to help the client learn and adapt to the new system. The second case indicates a basic social difficulty or deficit that exacerbates the difficulties inherent in immigration, and therefore counselors need deeper understanding of the individual's competency and of the intrafamilial system and interventions that target this system.

Independence and the Self

In Western societies, where individuals are raised to achieve an independent self and personality, psychological and social dependency is considered to be a sort of immaturity. In collective/authoritarian societies independence has a different and sometimes opposite meaning. Emotional interconnectedness, conformity and submissiveness to norms and values, and loyalty to the familial and social authority are among the indicators of maturity. When viewed according to the Western meaning of dependence, many Arab/Muslim clients may meet the criteria of the DSM-IV criteria for "dependent personality disorder," although they are fully functional in their own societies. For instance, Fisek and Kagitcibasi (1999) warned counselors of misdiagnosing the interconnectedness and familial-self of Turkish people as emotional fusion, immaturity, or developmental arrest. Independency and lack of conformity are considered a kind of carelessness or egoism in Arab/Muslim societies and are recipes for recurrent conflicts and social rejection.

These cross-cultural differences concerning independence have important psychological implications with regard to the meaning of the self. Many measures of self-concept and self-esteem in fact measure constructs that have different meanings. When an Arab/Muslim client expresses himself, it is the collective self that is expressed, including familial needs, interests, norms, attitudes, and values. Low or high self-esteem has to do with the familial social status and with the attitude of the family toward the client. To enhance such self-esteem, counselors need to help create a new familial order rather than change the client's personal attitude toward the self.

Western clinicians need to be aware of the fact that independence and the self, like intelligence and social competency, are culture-bound constructs. Therefore, when working with Arab/Muslim immigrants, they need to understand and assess these constructs within a culturally sensitive framework.

CONSTRUCTS FOR ASSESSMENT: WORLDVIEW AND ATTACHMENT

The constructs that should be the targets of assessment in the Arab/Muslim case stem from the psychosocial dynamic of the Arab/Muslim personality. As shown in the previous chapter, it is the intrafamilial domain that is the key to under-standing the behavior and experience of Arab/Muslim clients, because it is within this domain that conflicts and coping are taking place. Counselors and therapists are encouraged to invest in understanding the client's experience within the family, the values and attitudes that direct the family life, the social coping strategies the client uses to cope with her distresses, and the functionality of these strategies. These constructs should be the main foci of assessment and are not less relevant than intrapsychic constructs such as IQ, self-concept, un-conscious conflicts, or defense mechanisms.

In the multicultural counseling literature, *worldview* and *acculturation* are among the most used constructs mentioned in the context of understanding the client (Dana, 1993; Grieger & Ponterotto, 1995; Ibrahim, Ohnishi, & Wilson, 1994). *Worldview* is considered as the "lens" through which people interpret their world. *Acculturation* is reflected in psychological changes that occur in individuals as a result of their interaction with other cultures. Grieger and Pont-erotto (1995) identified six components of worldview and acculturation that can be usefully examined in the context of counseling assessment:

1) the client's level of psychological mindedness (defined as familiarity with the Western middle-class concept of the term);
2) the family's level of psychological mindedness;
3) the client's/family's attitude toward counseling;
4) the client's level of acculturation;
5) the family's level of acculturation; and
6) the family's attitude toward acculturation.

Sue (1978) postulated that one's worldview determines how one perceives one's relationship to the world: people, institutions, nature, and things. He iden-tified different worldviews based on a person's locus of control and responsibil-ity. Internal locus of control and of responsibility is common among middle-class whites, while an external locus is common among African Americans.

Since Arab/Muslim clients may be very diverse, and in order to avoid stere-otypic attitudes, counselors and therapists who work with Arab/Muslim immi-grants need to assess the worldview and acculturation of the client and of the family. Actually, understanding these components of worldview and accultura-tion helps counselors assess the level of differentiation between the client's and the family's worldview, on the one hand, and the level of Westernization of each of them, on the other. Put in another way, counselors and therapists need to assess the client's level of psychological individuation from the family, and the family's level of traditionalism or strictness. As discussed in Chapter 5, the client's level of individuation actually shows the balance between social and private layers of his personality. The social layer of the less individuated clients typically occupies a larger portion of their personality and vice versa. Once the client is found to be traditional—and therefore possessing a collective personality—then clinicians need to assess the efficacy of the social-cultural coping skills within the family and society (Dwairy, 1998a, 2002a).

In order to assess the level of psychological individuation of a client, and the level of traditionalism and strictness of the family, counselors may employ some scales of worldview (e.g., Scale to Assess Worldview; see Ibrahim & Khan, 1987), or a semistructured interview (e.g., Berg-Cross & Chinen, 1995). Since introducing these instruments is beyond the scope of this chapter, I will simply suggest applying one of the main ideas of Berg-Cross and Chinen (1995) in the intake interview: Inquire into the client's and the family's worldview in parallel. When the client has been asked about herself in terms of her own concerns, needs, attitudes, values, manners, copings, and goals, the counselor should then ask about her family in the same terms. For instance, after asking the client about what gives her satisfaction in life, the counselor might ask, "And how is it for your family? What makes them satisfied?" Or when the client is asked about her attitudes or plans, the counselor might ask, "And what does your family think about this issue? How did they react to your plans? Can you identify some diversity in their reactions?" Based on the answers to these questions, the counselor will be able to assess the worldviews of the client and the family, and the level of differentiation or individuation of the client.

Arab/Muslim clients are very much influenced by their families, and it is therefore a must to interview the family in order to understand more about the dynamics and values of the family. Not infrequently this interview provides a different, or sometimes opposite, perspective from that described by the client. A similar interview strategy may be implemented with the family as with the client. Counselors may inquire about the family's needs, concerns, attitudes, and values, and then ask the family, "And how is it for the client?" "What is her attitude toward these needs (concerns, attitudes, values)?"

This strategy of interviewing may help the counselor locate the client and the family on the collectivism dimension. This task is very important in order to plan the intervention that fits the specific client and family (as will be shown in Chapter 9).

THE ASSESSMENT TOOLS

Psychological tests as well as the formal clinical setting are unfamiliar to Arab/Muslim immigrants. Typically, these clients approach counseling and psychotherapy after they have tried to get help from family members, traditional healers, or a medical doctor. They expect to get advice or directives. For many Arab/Muslim clients, the psychological test situation, where they are asked to respond to standardized stimuli in a standardized way, is a strange and confusing experience.

If their original social background was very directive and controlling, many Arab/Muslim clients feel confused and discomforted when exposed to projective tests. In these tests clients are exposed to vague stimuli in response to which they are expected to freely project their perceptions, attitudes, and feelings. In the Rorschach test they are exposed to inkblots and asked to tell what they see. In the Thematic Apperception Test (TAT) they are asked to compose stories for a series of pictures. In other projective tests clients are asked to complete sentences or to give free associations to some words. In all these tests the psychological world of clients is expected to be projected symbolically in their responses, which allows the psychologist to interpret them and learn about the client's internal world. Because of the nondirective nature of these tests, the anxiety level of Arab respondents is increased, and thus they may display signs of withdrawal or a narrowing of their range of responses. This withdrawal and anxiety is situational and may indicate the client's real response in a vague nondirective situation, but it should not be considered as a personality trait or dynamic. A similar response should be expected in other vague or ambiguous situations such as when "free association" or "nondirective therapy" is implemented.

Many test stimuli, such as TAT pictures, represent Western people and culture that are alien to the Arab/Muslim client. Because these stimuli are expected to reflect Western related experiences, some variations of the TAT pictures have been developed for African Americans (Thompson, 1949) and for Hispanics (Costantino, Malgaday, & Vasquez, 1981). The TAT pictures do not fit the real Arab/Muslim experience either. For example, this is what a 13-year-old Arab Bedouin boy said about TAT picture #4, which shows an angry man and a woman holding him: "This is a young man with his girlfriend coming out of a cinema; he wants to go to a pub, but she does not. He leaves her and goes into the pub for a beer." Of course, ideas such as girlfriend, cinema, pub, and beer are far from being part of the Bedouin experience, and the theme of leaving a lover so easily is borrowed from the stereotypical image of Western youth in Bedouin eyes. This story may reveal more about his image of Westerners than about the personal experience of that client. The alien nature of the picture for some Arab/Muslim clients may be the reason behind a poor, narrow, unorganized, or confused response, or the reason behind a "rejection" response. Attribution of these kinds of responses to the client's personality is considered to be a kind of misinterpretation, and it may have dangerous consequences such as pathologizing a normal client.

Obviously, responses to projective tests should be interpreted within each culture. In a comparison which I made between the performance of 16-year-old

Arab students and their Western counterparts on the Rorschach test (reported by Levitt and Truumaa, 1972), Arab students showed lower productivity (low R—17.2 versus 20.8), higher abstraction (high W—35 versus 21.9), lower stereotypic perception (low P—4.5 versus 5.3), and higher infantile anxiety (higher shading). Similarly, based on my clinical observation, adult Arab/Muslim traditional clients seem to score lower than American clients on productivity (R) and imagination (M) and higher on concrete perception (F%). However, when Western psychologists interpret the responses of an Arab or Muslim immigrant according to the American norms of the Rorschach test, they may mistakenly attribute lower productivity, higher abstraction, less stereotypic perception, higher infantile anxiety, and higher concrete perception and limited imagination to the individual client, rather than recognizing these as cultural characteristics that may surface in the responses to a projective test. Because of these cross-cultural differences, De Vos and Boyer (1989) suspected the validity of using the Rorschach test in the cases of Algerian Arab/Muslims and other collective ethnicities, and stressed the need for flexible interpretation of the test. They claimed that they do not believe in quantitative analyses of percentages and mechanical determinations of ratios in interpretation. They highlighted the importance of understanding the culture's normative patterns and interpreting the responses within that culture.

The aforementioned reservations concerning the norms of the Rorschach's test apply to nearly all other tests. The performance of Arab students in Bender-Gestalt and Draw-a-Person tests is similar to that of Americans until age 7; after that, the Arab scores show a comparative decline. At age 10 to 11, the performance of Arabs is equivalent to that of 8-year-old American children. This lag is explained by the lack of graphic and art experience Arab children receive at home and at school in comparison with their American counterparts (Dwairy, 1998a). The clinical observation of the author is that the performance of illiterate traditional Arab/Muslim adults is very similar to that of retarded children. This observation may open the eyes of counselors to the possibility that an Arab client's performance may be misleading, and misdiagnosis will thus be avoided.

Some of the test tasks are seen as childish by many Arab/Muslim clients, who therefore display signs of rejection or humiliation. These signs may appear when the client is asked the easy questions of an intelligence test or when he is asked to do tasks that are associated with children, such as block design or drawings. Some clients express themselves by saying, "I am not a child," or, "Do you think I'm that crazy?" When these tasks are misunderstood by the client, the rapport with and confidence in the counselor may be endangered. Sometimes such a misunderstanding may constitute the client's reason for quitting counseling, as one client did—but not before saying that he was a respected manager who does all the accounting for a big company.

During the early period of my professional experience, right after I had opened the first psychological services center for the Arab population in Israel, I needed to test a 62-year-old Arab/Muslim man who suffered from fears and phobias. In accordance with my formal Western academic training, I asked the secretary to invite him to "two sessions for psychological diagnosis" during which I planned to administer a formal battery of tests. When he arrived for the first session, I invited him into my room and gave him the formal instructions for the Bender-Gestalt and then the drawing tests. After hesitating for a long time, he picked up the pencil and drew some graphics, but he seemed anxious and confused. After a while he became nervous and displayed clear signs of rejection. I documented every sign of nervousness and rejection, especially during the drawing of the male and the female figures. When these signs worsened in their intensity, I asked him if anything was bothering him, and he replied, "Yes, I am anxious because I have an appointment to be examined by a doctor." As a 25-year-old psychologist, not yet a doctor, dressed in casual clothes, it was not easy to convince him that I was the one who was supposed to examine him. In spite of everything, he proceeded to respond to the TAT test. When the session ended, he said, "Doctor, next session I will bring a flute." When he noticed my signs of surprise, he added, "Today we drew and told stories; next time I will play on the flute and you will sing." At this point I realized that I should have explained to him the rationale of the tests and of psychotherapy in order that he would not confuse the tests with play or leisure time. Although it was late, I gave him the necessary explanations and he started therapy.

The misunderstanding between Western-oriented therapists and Arab/Muslim clients is not limited to the assessment stage, but rather continues throughout therapy. During therapy, it became obvious to me that the fears of this 62-year-old man were associated with his manhood and with a serious conflict situation with his domineering wife. Nevertheless, his traditional rationale for therapy or treatment was much more influential than my therapy. The "talk therapy" did not seem to meet his expectations of real dramatic action; therefore, while we were setting the next appointment, he said, "Next time I will bring my wife with me."

I asked, "Why do you think you want to bring her?"

He said, "I will drum (*attbolha,* beat as a drum) her here [indicating the middle of the room], in front of you."

I was astonished and said, "Why would you want to beat her?"

He answered, "Don't you think it would help?" and continued to explain to me why he thought that he would overcome his fears if he did something that would prove his manhood, such as beating his wife, in front of his psychologist.

This case among many others may open the eyes of counselors and therapists to the need for orienting the clients to the tests and to the counseling process.

EMPLOYING THE PHYSICAL ENVIRONMENT
IN PSYCHOSOCIAL ASSESSMENT

Arab/Muslims living in the East are attached to their villages, houses, and lands. Their mobility is very limited. Typically they are raised in and continue to inhabit the same place for generations. If for any reason they leave their village, they adopt the name of the village or town of origin. Many Arab/Muslim family names are therefore linked to their places of origin; for instance the Nasrawi family is a family that originated in Nasra (Nazareth) and the Baghdadi family came from Baghdad. This association between the family name or identity and the village or city of origin represents the psychosocial connectedness between Arab/Muslims and their physical environment. This attachment to a place is considered to be part of the identity, honor, and esteem of the family. Within this culture, selling the family's land or leaving its village is an almost damning action. In the rural areas of Egypt, for instance, selling land is condemned and is considered parallel to giving up the honor and dignity of the family.

The psychology literature is rich in concepts that describe the psychological relationship between the individual and social environments: Attachment, identification, separation-individuation, and projection are just a few among many concepts. Conversely, "transitional object" (Winnicott, 1953) may be the only concept in the psychology literature that describes a psychological relationship with one's physical environment. This tendency to ignore the physical environment seems to be a result of the process of separating or individuation through which individuals in the West pass. The individual there is an independent entity that is separate from the family as well as from the physical environment. This separation is associated with the high mobility of Westerners. Conversely, in the East individuals continue to be integrated within the family as well as in their physical environment.

I have developed an assessment technique called Talking About Significant Objects (TASO) (Dwairy, 2001, 2003), based on the assumption that our physical environments are not simply abiotic, but rather are charged with memories and emotions that are related to significant intrafamilial experiences in the past and present. Wedding rings, necklaces, private items, books, gifts, clothes, kitchen tools, items of furniture—all can be significant objects that symbolize a significant relationship, event, or experience. When a counselor asks the client to bring an object that has special meaning for him to the next session, actually, the client is reassociated to the physical environment and eventually to hidden or remote significant intimate intrafamilial experiences. For several days until the next meeting the client is expected to spend a lot of time retrieving past experiences and thinking about the meaning of the items in the physical environment. When the next session comes, the therapist may ask the client to talk about the item he has brought and its significance and meaning. When necessary, the therapist asks: "How did you choose this item? What came up in your mind while you were exploring the items around it? What made you chose this? What meaning does it have? What memories are associated with this item? What happened? Who was there? How did you feel? How did you cope?" Usually, the conversation about the chosen item reveals a central conflict in the client's life and the way it was handled.

Counselors and therapists may ask the client to bring different items to each session in order to cover different aspects of the client's life and experiences. The objects that the client brings to the sessions may be considered as objects of projection, similar to TAT or Rorschach cards. Keeping in mind that many Arab/Muslim clients are not psychologically separated from their physical environment, one can appreciate that talking about a significant object is a process that is much beyond a projection process. When the individual's self is not separate from the social or from the physical environment, talking about a significant object is, in fact, talking directly about the self and the family.

Therapeutic conversation about the objects that the client brings to the session introduces into the counseling or therapeutic process the significant memories and experiences of the client within the family, including bonds, conflicts, and losses. This technique, in fact, bypasses the barrier that many counselors face when they ask an Arab/Muslim client to talk about his self or inner world. For these clients, talking about a concrete object is much easier, and, in the last analysis, it constitutes talking about the self. The TASO technique has a therapeutic use beyond mere assessment, which will be discussed in Chapter 11.

The meaning of some core psychological constructs, such as intelligence and independence, is substantially different among Arab/Muslims. The mind is associated with control, morals, and values much more than with logic and reasoning. Emotional interdependence, conformity and submissiveness to norms and values, and loyalty to the familial are among the indicators of maturity. Counselors who work with Arab/Muslim immigrants need to know the social competency of these clients within both their original culture and the new Western culture.

SUMMARY

To understand an Arab/Muslim client, counselors should assess certain uncommon constructs such as worldview, acculturation, level of psychological individuation of the client, the balance between social and private layers of personality, and the level of traditionalism and strictness of the family. In addition, the performance of the Arab/Muslim clients in psychological tests should be understood within a culturally sensitive approach. Inquiring about the family values, norms, and experiences and the discrepancy between those of the family and those of the client is very important. This target may be achieved by directing the conversation accordingly and by talking about objects from the client's physical environment.

Chapter 7

Diagnosis and Psychopathology of Arabs/Muslims

The Western nosology of mental health is based on the reductionistic approach that considers individuals as independent entities, makes a clear distinction between psychological and organic/somatic disorders, and identifies specific and distinct psychological disorders such as anxiety, depression, dissociation, or psychosis. This classification system attributes a unique etiology, course, and treatment to each of these disorders. Is the Western nosology applicable also to members of the Arab/Muslim culture, in which the individuals are not individuated from the collective, the mind and body are not distinct entities, and the internal constructs of personality (emotions, thoughts, self, superego) are not distinct one from the other?

The Arab/Muslim theory of mental health is very holistic, to the extent that it intertwines supernatural entities with people's lives. The Arabic term for mental illness or insanity, *jinnoon*, is derived from the noun *jinn* that means devil or demon. *Jinnoon* is a person's state when a *jinn* possesses the body. Abnormal behavior, according to this theory, occurs as a result of possession that is caused either by a sin that the person or family member has committed or by the evil eye of someone who possesses feelings of jealousy. Many Arabs/Muslims believe in this theory, and they understand how the psychological disorder influences how they cope with these disorders and how they seek help, accordingly. Many of them seek healers, or *shekhes*, to exorcise the *jinn* or to undo the influence of the evil eye through amulets or certain rituals.

By attributing mental illness to external evil entities, Arabs/Muslims free the afflicted person from any responsibility for her deviant behavior. This conceptualization of mental illness fits the traditional strict sociocultural system according to which feelings and drives such as aggression and sex should be suppressed. Within this system, being possessed by a *jinn* actually permits the individual to act out these forbidden drives, without taking responsibility for her resulting actions (El-Islam, 1982). According to the Arab/Muslim theory, the only responsibility the client has is to avoid sinning, and, after such an illness, to submit herself to religious healers (*shekhes*) in order to exorcize the *jinn.* These beliefs, of course, prevent the client from playing an active role in psychotherapy based on self-responsibility and on "working on the self."

The *jinnoon* label is applied to a variety of chronic disorders, including mental retardation, and neurotic and psychotic disorders. When the disorder is precipitated by a stressful event, the case is labeled *inheyar a'sabi* (nervous breakdown). This disorder is reactive and involves a variety of symptoms such as anxiety, depression, dissociation, psychosis, and also somatic symptoms. These two "diagnostic" labels, *jinnoon* and *inheyar a'sabi*, are global, with no differentiation between subcategories as in Western nosology. Mixed rather than distinct syndromes seem to be a very common clinical picture among Arabs/Muslims. Therefore, serious precautions should be taken when applying the distinct categories described in DSM-IV to Arab/Muslim clients.

Many epidemiological studies have found a high intercorrelation between anxiety, depression, and somatic symptoms. When two or more disorders (such as somatoform disorder and depression) are identified in a client according to Western categories, comorbidity between the originally distinct disorders is claimed (or considered) to be present (Simon & Von Korff, 1991). Ethnographic studies provide much evidence for mixed somatic-affective syndromes. The most prominent example is neurasthenia, which is a mixture of depression and somatic symptoms, such as fatigue and weakness. This diagnosis is extremely common in China, where Kleinman (1986) found that 87% of neurasthenic patients met the criteria for major depression, and 69% met the criteria for anxiety disorder. Clinicians and researchers working in the United States with refugees from Southeast Asia and Central America have found a high co-occurrence of post-traumatic stress syndrome, depressive, and dissociative symptoms, which led Eisenbruch (1991) to propose a new category, "cultural bereavement," as a diagnosis that more fully captures the mixed syndrome. Okasha and his colleagues reported that the psychosis common in Egypt is very polymorphic, involving acute excitement, depression, delusions, and hallucinations (Okasha, Seif El Dawla, Khalil, & Saad, 1993).

Since culture has a profound influence on the experience and expression of symptoms, the *DSM-IV Sourcebook* (Vol. 3) allocated the sixth section to cultural issues (APA, 1997). This section points to cultural considerations in various diagnostic categories, including somatoform, anxiety, mood, psychotic, dissociative, sexual, eating, and personality disorders. The considerations mentioned in the section are related mainly to minorities who live in the United States. I focus here on those that pertain clearly to the more traditional Arab/Muslim immigrants who are less assimilated and still maintain a collective style of life.

SOMATOFORM DISORDERS

Somatization is one common widespread feature mentioned in the literature dealing with psychological disorders of many non-Western cultures. It is a term that describes psychological conflicts and distresses that are expressed in bodily complaints. It implies a clear distinction between mind and body, and assumes the existence of two distinct domains of disorders. It is characteristic of the Western dualist culture to separate the psychological and physical components of a distressing experience. In fact, Western culture has given primacy to the psychological domain and has psychologized some of the mind-body experiences, dissociating them from the body.

In a holistic mind-body culture such as the Arab/Muslim one, distress is expressed in both mental and physical complaints. Because of the absence of a distinct domain for the self, somatic complaints are sometimes the only expression of distress. In addition, because complaints about fears or sadness are not encouraged in the Arab/Muslim culture and may evoke criticism rather than sympathy or support, physical complaints become the legitimate and less costly way of expressing personal problems (Budman, Lipson, & Meleis, 1992; Racy, 1977). The term somatization is misleading because in these cultures there are no distinct and pure psychological distresses in the first place, so therefore there is no place for somatization. In the last analysis almost all the syndromes found among collective people such as Arabs/Muslims are somatoform. Thus this category does not advance clinical understanding when it is applied; a diagnosis of somatoform disorder is almost useless in relation to Arabs/Muslims.

ANXIETY DISORDERS

Two culture-specific features are related to anxiety disorder among Arabs/Muslims: purification and *weswas*. Islam orders Muslims to pray five times a day. Each prayer includes specific verses and sayings and ritualistic movements. Before each prayer Muslims should wash their heads, face, and extremities in a ritualistic sequence. These purification rites meet many of the criteria of DSM-IV for obsessive-compulsive disorder (OCD). Indeed, Okasha and his colleagues (Okasha, 1999; Okasha, Saad, Khalil, Seif El Dawla, & Yehia, 1994) found that the OCD manifestations in Egypt are colored by Islamic religious rituals and beliefs. Many OCD subjects (68%) have obsessive thoughts about contamination and infection and many (63%) are preoccupied with cleaning, washing, purification, and praying. Interestingly, and in contrast to one of the DSM-IV criteria of OCD, most OCD subjects in the Egyptian study did not recognize the absurdity of their symptoms. This overlap between Islamic rites and OCD makes the differential diagnosis difficult. One major issue that may help to distinguish one from the other is that Islamic rules offer clear alternative rites if some of the rituals or prayers are missed. Therefore, missing a ritual should not evoke anxiety. The OCD client, however, feels high anxiety once he misses a ritual, which intensifies the OCD symptoms.

Weswas is a culture-bound syndrome among Arabs/Muslims. It means ruminating on bad thoughts, which the client does not attribute to the self but rather to an external entity such as a *jinn* or devil, thus enabling her to avoid responsibility and guilt feelings. Typically, the content of these thoughts concerns forbidden things, such as sexual or aggressive acts, that are considered sinful. These thoughts are attributed to the devil, and therefore one is directed to look for refuge in God by uttering the saying: *Aʿauth be Allah men al-shaytan al-rajeem* [I take refuge in God away from the devil]. Clinicians who are unfamiliar with the *weswas* syndrome may consider the subject to have delusional thoughts, leading to a mistaken misdiagnosis of psychosis. Giving a psychodynamic interpretation to the client, so that she will become aware of her repressed forbidden wishes, typically threatens the client and evokes high anxiety, which may make her quit counseling (see Matta's case in Chapter 9). It is therefore recommended that the counselor refer the traditional client to religious leaders or healers, *shekhes*, for advice. Uncovering forbidden repressed needs can be helpful only when the client is both individuated and strong enough to handle and deal with these needs. Otherwise counselors should avoid this type of revelation and look for traditional/religious ways of obtaining relief (see Dwairy, 1997b, concerning how to address repressed needs).

MOOD DISORDERS

Although depression is considered to be the most common disorder in Western cultures, it is not even found in the lexicon of some Asian cultures. Some scholars regard depression as a disorder of the Western world (e.g., Marsella, 1978), which lacks universal applicability (Fernando, 1988). Despite the fact that depression is an affective and mood disorder manifested in dysphoria, it has significant associated somatic components, such as appetite and weight change, sleep disturbances, psychomotor agitation or retardation, fatigue, motor tension, autonomic hyperactivity, and recurrent thoughts of death. Further insight into the cultural patterning of depression can be obtained from studies made using the Center for Epidemiologic Studies of Depression (CES-D) scale. This is a measure that includes items from previously established scales in order to study the epidemiology of depressive symptomatology. The 20-item scale assesses the occurrence and persistence of the following symptoms in a one-week period: depressed mood, feelings of guilt and worthlessness, psychomotor retardation, loss of appetite, and sleep disturbance. Radloff (1977) described factor analyses of CES-D that yielded a consistent dimensional structure comprising four factors that she labeled *depressed affect, somatic complaints, positive affect, and interpersonal difficulties.* Interestingly, factor analyses of CES-D from samples of Chinese Americans (Kuo, 1984; Ying, 1988) and Hispanic Americans (Garcia, & Marks, 1989; Guarneccia, Good, & Kleinman, 1990) yielded three factors in which depressed affect and somatic complaints factors were combined. Factor analysis among American Indian samples revealed a three-factor solution with a strong "general" factor that included depressed, somatic, and interpersonal items (Baron, Manson, & Ackerson, 1990; Manson, Ackerson, & Dick, 1990). The correlation between the depressed affect and somatic complaints factors was so high (.90) that they should be considered indistinguishable (Manson, 1997). If this is the case among non-Western ethnic groups in the United States, it is reasonable to assume that the overlap between the depressive mood and somatic symptoms will be greater among citizens of non-Western countries.

The greatest difficulty in diagnosing non-Western depressive clients lies in determining the presence of *dysphoria*: depressed mood or loss of interest or pleasure. Some scholars argue that the expressions of emotions are essentially cultural artifacts (Rosaldo, 1984), and that non-Western populations do not differentiate somatic from affective complaints and are therefore predisposed to report depressive affect in somatic rather than psychological terms. In addition, *dysphoria* is typically defined as "self-awareness to personal emotions" (e.g., "*I* feel blue," or "Life means nothing to *me*") (Manson, 1997), which explains the absence of dysphoria among clients from a collective holistic background, where the self does not exist as an independent entity.

Various cultures encourage or suppress certain emotions. For instance, the Palestinian Arab/Muslim culture discourages families of martyred soldiers from displaying sorrow, while the Iranian Arab/Muslim culture encourages displays of extreme sadness and sorrow (Good & Good, 1982). The expression of affect is thus culture-related. A comparison between depressive patients in Egypt, India, and Great Britain revealed that the Egyptian Arab/Muslim and Indian patients displayed more anxiety and somatic symptoms than did the British. Anxiety was displayed in 99%, and somatic symptoms in 87%, of the Egyptian sample (Abd El-Gawad, 1995). In addition, suicidal thoughts in the Egyptian depressives were relatively high compared with the low rates of suicide and attempted suicide. Guilt feelings among the Egyptian sample were relatively few. Okasha (1999) reported similar findings. He claims that Egyptian depressed patients mask their affect with multiple somatic symptoms that occupy the foreground, and the affective component of their illness recedes into the background. Similar results were reported among Turkish depressive patients: more somatic symptoms, more suicidal thoughts, and a low suicide rate (see Tuncer,

1995). In Sudan, Baasher (1962) reported similar characteristics of depression among Sudanese patients and noticed that the fear of breaking the rules or shaming themselves and their families was more dominant among these patients than feelings of individual responsibility and guilt. These observations in different cultures suggest that distress is typically expressed by people in non-Western cultures in multiple symptoms, in which depressive mood is not necessarily a dominant component.

PSYCHOTIC DISORDERS

The World Health Organization (1973, 1979) conducted international studies in nine countries and found a significant similarity as well as substantial variations in schizophrenic symptoms. It has been reported that acute reactive psychosis is more prevalent in Africa (Lin & Kleinman, 1988). Hallucinations of all types were more prevalent among patients from Africa and Asia than among Western patients (Ndetei & Vadher, 1984). Studies in the United States revealed that Mexican Americans display a more florid degree of psychotic symptoms than do non-Hispanic white schizophrenic patients (Fabrega, Swartz, & Wallace, 1968). The World Health Organization studies, as well as others, have been substantially buttressed by the evidence that schizophrenia in non-Western societies is characterized by an onset precipitated by stress (e.g., divorce or loss), a polymorphic picture that may include schizophrenic, affective, and neurotic symptoms during an acute and short course; most patients recovered rapidly within a year (Cooper, Jablensky, & Sartorius, 1990; Murphy & Ramman, 1971; Waxler, 1977). This clinical picture may validate the presence of a special psychotic diagnostic category.

Arab/Muslim schizophrenics in Egypt were compared by Abd El-Gawad (1995) with those in Great Britain and the United States. The symptoms within each group were ranked according to their frequency. He found significant differences in the symptoms' rank; that is, symptoms such as incongruity of affect, thought withdrawal, thought block, apathy, and incoherence ranked higher in the Egyptian patients than in the other two samples. Delusions ranked second in the U.S. sample, but tenth in the Egyptian one. Okasha and his colleagues (Okasha, Seif El Dawla, et al., 1993) studied the manifestations of psychosis in Egypt. Delusions, depression, excitement, hallucinations, worrying, delayed sleep, and irritability were the most common presenting symptoms of Egyptian psychotic patients. The most frequent diagnosis among the psychotic Egyptian patients was brief reactive psychosis, with polymorphic acute symptoms precipitated by stress, and with rapid recovery. The onset of acute psychosis occurred within 5 days in 68% of patients. A stressor preceded the onset of psychotic symptoms in 74% of the patients, and correlated positively with a favorable prognosis at the one-year follow-up. During this same follow-up period, 64% of the patients had fully remitted. The social and clinical outcomes of the patients were not correlated with family psychiatric history. El-Islam (1979) reported that Arab schizophrenics belonging to extended families had fewer malevolent manifestations and were found to be less prone to deterioration into affectively blunted and withdrawn states than those belonging to nuclear families. All these research findings help clinicians who work with Arab/Muslim immigrants appreciate the special features of schizophrenia among this population that deviate a bit from the DSM-IV criteria for schizophrenia.

The uniqueness of psychosis among Arabs/Muslims led three psychiatrists from Tunisia, Morocco and Algeria to edit a "manual of psychiatry for the North African practitioner" (Douki, Moussaoui, & Kocha, 1987, cited in Al-Issa, 1989), in which they reported psychotic categories unique to the North African Arabs. One of these categories, called "psychosis of passion," includes erotomania (the delusion that one is loved by someone else) and delusions of jealousy and revenge.

Concepts of reality, cultural beliefs, and metaphoric descriptions should be taken into consideration during the diagnostic stage of Arab/Muslim clients. Sufism (a branch of Islam), for instance, considers the objective reality to be the unreal one. For them, the "real" reality can be reached only through meditating (or trance state), which brings the Sufist closer to God. This concept of reality contradicts the essence of "reality testing" that is the basis of the diagnosis of psychosis. Many cultural beliefs may be considered to be delusions by clinicians who are not aware of these cultural issues. In a study about the effect of the evil eye in Lebanon, for example, 81.3% of the mothers reported that they believed that the evil eye had had a harmful effect on their infants (Harfouche, 1981). Arabs/Muslims perform several rituals that are intended to protect them from the evil eye—some of which may seem bizarre—such as incantation and the use of amulets, blue beads, or a horseshoe (Donaldson, 1981; Harfouche, 1981). These beliefs and rituals may be pathologized, while conversely other pathological delusions and rituals may sometimes be normalized and misattributed to cultural beliefs. Metaphoric descriptions of the experience of an Arab/Muslim patient may add more confusion and misunderstanding to the assessment of the reality testing. As an example, one expression that is commonly used by Arabs/Muslims is "*hwo sammelly badani.*" This expression literally means "he poisoned my body," while the intended meaning is "he made me nervous." An unaware therapist who hears a woman saying, "Yesterday my husband became furious and poisoned my body," may misinterpret this as delusion or as a homicide attempt (see Chapter 11 concerning metaphors).

DISSOCIATIVE DISORDERS

To my knowledge, there are no empirical reports about the prevalence of dissociative disorders in the Arab countries. Clinical impressions suggest that dissociation between the self and the body (e.g., somatoform disorders or possession) is more common among Arabs than dissociation of the self. Multiple personality disorder seems to be very rare or nonexistent in Arab society. Considering the fact that the self among Arabs does not individuate completely and does not exist as an independent entity, it is reasonable to assume that a split of the (nonexistent) self is not feasible. Therefore, multiple personality disorder is not likely to occur. On the other hand, possession and trance state seem to be common among Arabs/Muslims. Many psychosocial disorders are conceptualized as a state of possession. *Zar* is a term that is used to refer to several mental illnesses. It is a class of spirits that is believed typically to possess women. Treatment of these illnesses is by means of a *zar* ceremony in which a trance state is induced by a healer who tries to convince the *zar* spirit to leave the body (Al-Sabaie, 1989). During the course of the illness, as well as during the *zar* ceremony, the patient experiences dissociative states in which she expresses forbidden aggressive or sexual acts, believing that these are the responsibility of the spirit, and takes no responsibility for these acts. Trance states, as when a *zar* ceremony is held, are thought to be healing events (El-Islam, 1982).

SEXUAL DISORDERS

Paraphilias (deviant sexual behavior), sexual dysfunctions, and other sexual disorders that are defined in DSM-IV may not be applicable to Arabs/Muslims, because what is considered deviant in one culture may well be regarded as nonproblematic in another. Pedophilia in the Western sense could not be applied to members of Arab/Muslim societies that legitimize marriage of men or boys to girls less than 18 years old. Sexual relationships before marriage, although accepted in the West, are strictly forbidden in Arab/Muslim communities. The liberal attitude toward homosexuality, which has been adopted in the West as a part of the general liberal attitude and individualistic freedom of choice, would not be countenanced in many Arab/Muslim societies, where the religious laws as well as the state laws severely punish any manifestation of homosexuality.

The restrictions pertaining to relationships between male and female Arab/Muslim children lead to homosexual behavior and masturbation as part of the sexual games that usually take place during the course of the sexual development of children and adolescents. Homosexual behavior may occur in the Arab/Muslim society either as a sexual game or as exploitation of younger boys by older boys or men. Unlike in the West, homosexual behavior in these societies is usually situational and is not necessarily associated with sexual identity or stable sexual preference. Very little is known about homosexual behavior or masturbation among Arab/Muslim women. The revelation of masturbatory experiences by female clients during the course of therapy is typically accompanied by much shame and guilt.

Some cultural styles of communication among Arabs/Muslims may mislead the Western observer. Physical expression of warmth and friendship is practiced within the same gender, but almost prohibited between genders. When Arabs meet after a long absence, men hug and kiss each other, and women do the same with women. It is not uncommon to see two male friends holding hands in public, or one putting a hand on the shoulder of the other. Brides in many Arab areas hold women's parties in which women dance with other women. All of these socially accepted behaviors are the result of the strict segregation of genders rather than an indication of homosexuality.

As a result of the rigid restrictions on sexual behavior, especially among women, it is reasonable to assume a high prevalence of sexual problems related to guilt, anxiety, and inhibition. Clinical impressions suggest a high prevalence of vaginismus among Arab/Muslim women that is usually considered an indication of modesty. When it occurs in the early days of marriage, it is considered normal. The bride is encouraged by her family to keep withstanding the pain. If she continues to be reluctant, the husband may marry another woman. Because Arab/Muslim societies in general do not treat men and women equally, many disorders of sexual inhibition are not considered disorders when they occur in Arab/Muslim women. For instance, what the West refers to as hypoactive sexual desire disorder, female sexual arousal disorder, and female orgasmic disorder are considered normal conditions by many Arabs/Muslims because women are assumed not to have sexual desires other than to meet their husbands' sexual needs. On the other hand, premature ejaculation is rarely considered to be a disorder for Arab/Muslim males. For some, it may even be considered a symbol of high sexual potency or overmasculinity. Erectile problems are the main issues that worry Arab/Muslim men. Erectile problems in men, as well as vaginismus problems in women, are the main sexual problems that receive attention in the Arab/Muslim society.

The cultural attitude of Arab/Muslim societies toward sexuality may explain much of the sexual dysfunction. Many sexual dysfunctions are the result of the impact of the wedding night. In some communities the whole extended family waits outside the bedroom until the consummation of the marriage. In these circumstances many men have found themselves unable to achieve erection. These circumstances also put much pressure on the bride because if she proves not to be a virgin she will be punished and divorced. Fortunately, these customs have ceased in urban areas, but the intervention and pressure of family on the young couple to conceive still exist.

EATING DISORDERS

Food in the Arab/Muslim culture is much more than just nutrition; it is a means of communication that indicates social relationships. Inviting a person to a meal and the acceptance of such an invitation means that both sides want to promote the relationship to a close and almost familial one. Providing food expresses love and warmth. Reluctance to accept an invitation to eat a meal with someone means rejecting the relationship. An idiom such as *"Akalna aésh wmalh sawa"* [we ate bread and salt together] expresses a deep bond between two Arab/Muslim people. Based on this social meaning and function of food, eating disorders are assumed to be associated with problems related to relationships with others more than to the body or the self. Furthermore, one can assume that, as long as the harmony within the family is maintained to the benefit of all, eating disorders among its members will remain uncommon. The mother-children relationship, regardless of the children's age, is built on the mother's feeding and preparing meals for them. Eagerness for their mother's cooking is one of the major ways in which adult children express their love to their mothers.

Anorexia nervosa and bulimia nervosa are considered to be culture-bound syndromes of Western society (Russell, 1993). It became common with the abundance and profusion of modern society, on the one hand, and the ideal of "thin is beautiful," on the other. In Arab/Muslim culture, thinness has been regarded as socially undesirable, whereas plumpness is regarded as a symbol of health and fertility (Nasser, 1988). In addition, the majority of Arabs/Muslims, who live in poverty and tend to suffer from malnutrition, associate "thin" with "poverty," and do not have the luxury of choosing their diet. Therefore, eating disorders among them are very rare (El-Sarrag, 1968).

Immigrants are usually influenced by the normative values of the hosting country, so one might expect that Arab/Muslim immigrants in the West would be influenced by the dieting and appearance norms of the new society. Abou-Saleh, Younis, and Karim (1998) considered anorexia to be a *culture-reactive syndrome* because it occurs mainly under conditions of rapid cultural change, and because it has an increased incidence in immigrant groups. One can assume that eating disorders may reflect the fact that the harmony of the family among Arab/Muslim immigrants is threatened and they are facing many cultural challenges.

Nasser (1986) studied eating disorders among 50 Egyptian female university students in London and 60 female students in Cairo universities. No evidence of anorexia or bulimia was found in the Cairo sample, but 12% of the sample in England met the criteria of bulimia nervosa. In the United Arab Emirates, Abou-Saleh and colleagues (1998) reported the first five cases of anorexia and attributed it to the increasing Westernization of the country. Based on these findings, practitioners in the West may expect to encounter cases of eating disorders among Arabs/Muslims.

PERSONALITY DISORDERS

Personality is a cultural product (Markus & Kitayama, 1998), and therefore clinicians should take culture into consideration when a psychological assessment is made. When the sociocultural background of Arabs/Muslims is denied, the collective, unindividuated personality (described in Chapter 5) may be considered as a dependent personality disorder because it meets the criteria for that disorder. Arabs/Muslims are emotionally dependent on their families; their self-esteem is dependent on family approval; they tend to care for their families more than for themselves; and they avoid making personal decisions that contradict the family will. Since Arab/Muslim minorities in the West may feel rejected, or at least that their culture is rejected by the majority, some may develop a defensive antisocial attitude and behavior that may be seen as an antisocial personality disorder, or a suspicious attitude that may be seen as a paranoid personality disorder.

Borderline personality disorder has been found in some instances to be the result of rapid cultural changes faced by individuals who lack adaptive skills (Murphy, 1982). Gorkin, Masalha, and Yatziv (1985) reported a different characteristic of borderline Arab clients as compared to Western clients: They are less schizoid and rarely experience a feeling of detachment and emptiness, and their acting-out of sexual or antisocial drives seems to be accompanied by feelings of enormous passion.

Alarcon and Foulks (1997) suggested applying the principle of *cultural contextualization* during the diagnostic process, that is, putting all criteria, evaluative techniques, or clinical approaches to the assessment of a given personality disorder category into cultural perspective. The context has to be derived from some understanding of the culture from which the individual comes to counseling. Assessment of any criterion (such as dependency) should therefore be relative to the norms within the client's culture.

SUMMARY

As compared to the reductionistic Western nosology represented in the DSM-IV, the psychological disorders among Arabs/Muslims tend to be mixed rather than distinct syndromes. Anxiety, depression, dissociation, and somatic symptoms are highly intercorrelated among Arabs/Muslims. To avoid misdiagnosis, practitioners who are familiar with the Western nosology of mental health are advised to be aware of the uniqueness of each diagnostic category among Arabs/ Muslims immigrants. Almost all the diagnostic categories are manifested in a unique clinical picture and course that need to be known to practitioners.

PART III

WORKING WITH ARAB AND MUSLIM CLIENTS IN THE UNITED STATES AND ABROAD

Based on cross-cultural differences in personality and psychopathology, psychotherapeutic strategies and techniques should be revised when working with Arab/Muslim clients. Psychotherapy and counseling that aim to help the client to fulfill himself or to "make what is unconscious conscious" may not fit Arab/Muslim clients whose personality is collective rather than individual. Sometimes these strategies may be counterproductive and work against the good of the client, as discussed in Chapters 8 and 9.

Chapter 10 focuses on therapy with Arab/Muslim women. Mental health of Arab/Muslim women is typically related to social oppression against women. Immigrant Arab/Muslim women may suffer from depression, isolation, and low self-esteem which may influence the whole family.

Interventions that restore order in the family, rather than order in the self, are recommended for Arab/Muslim immigrants. In some cases, clinicians need to avoid revealing some of the client's unconscious contents in order to avoid tough confrontation with the family. In these cases indirect therapy such as metaphor therapy, the subject of Chapter 11, is recommended.

Chapter 8

Limitations of Psychotherapeutic Approaches

Generally speaking, *psychopathology* is defined as a disorder in the intrapsychic domain. Psychotherapy is therefore designed and intended to restore the intrapsychic order in the individuated client. In relation to collective peoples, Western psychotherapeutic approaches are limited. These limitations concern the goals as well as the techniques of psychotherapy. Therapeutic goals such as self-actualization, making what is unconscious conscious, or becoming assertive may reveal forbidden needs and emotions and result in a confrontation between the client and his or her authoritarian and strict family, which the client is sure to lose (Dwairy, 1997b). Some therapeutic techniques, such as nondirective therapy or interpretation of the transference, are counterproductive (Dwairy, 1997c). This chapter will describe the limitations and the cultural barriers that face each psychotherapeutic approach and direct the reader concerning the elements that should or should not be applied in the case of Arab/Muslim immigrants.

TALK THERAPY ABOUT PERSONAL INTIMATE ISSUES

The main medium of psychotherapy is the conversation. Sue and Sue (1990) indicated the existence of very important cultural barriers in relation to the therapy of non-Western clients that involve insight and self-disclosure. Similar barriers may be faced when talk therapy is used to treat Arab/Muslim clients.

First, Arabs/Muslims come to therapy with the expectation of being given concrete practical advice, and cannot understand how talk may cure their symptoms, many of which are somatic.

Second, talk, for Arabs/Muslims, is a tool for social communication that is used to set demands or meet expectations and to please others rather than to express authentic genuine internal feelings or attitudes. For these reasons Arabs/Muslims find talking about intimate personal feelings in the therapeutic conversation difficult. Talk has little to do with internal communication, and therefore some clients seem to have no access to their own inner feelings and find it difficult to answer even common therapeutic questions such as "How do you feel?" Many reply to this question with an expected or desired answer such as "Thanks to God." Others may respond to this question with a vague answer, such as "regular" or "natural." Or when asked "how do you feel about your father?" may respond with a moral answer, such as "He is my father, of course I love him."

Finally, if they have to talk, Arab/Muslim clients are ready to talk about their symptoms, but they do not comprehend why they are asked about intimate or personal issues such as childhood, family relationships, or sexual experiences. In addition to these difficulties, each therapeutic approach has its own difficulties when applied to Arabs/Muslims.

PSYCHODYNAMIC APPROACH

Freud and his followers emphasize unconscious drives as the main factor in psychopathology and psychoanalysis. They therefore focus on the intrapsychic domain in order to make the unconscious content conscious and in the control of the ego. Since this kind of therapy assumes that familial and social influences are almost completely limited to the early years of life, it neglects them in the therapy of adults and focuses instead on the internalized objects.

The core of the psychodynamic therapy is the interpretation of transference. This interpretation is intended to bring the client to the realization that he is reenacting his relationships of the past with new objects in the present. This insight is supposed to enhance the client's reality testing, so that he realizes that he has no present reason to react in the way that he does. This realization may be true when the client has achieved psychological individuation and established an independent personality. In the case of the Arab/Muslim client, whose personality is collective and unindividuated and who continues in adulthood to be dependent and controlled by external factors, attributing the present distress solely to the past may be untrue, misleading, and unhelpful. The intrapsychic domain of Arabs/Muslims is not independent of the current familial and social domains; thus, it would be insufficient to create a new intrapsychic order while the other domains continue to be neglected or abused.

When the therapist and the clients are of opposite sexes, interpreting the transference that takes place in the therapeutic relationship may be problematic. Discussing feelings, especially positive feelings, with a member of the opposite sex may be too threatening or unacceptable for a client from a modest culture. The client may misunderstand such a course of action as a kind of harassment or molestation. Interpretation of transference in the therapeutic relationship can, therefore, only be done with extreme caution.

Psychoanalysis assumes that sexual or hostile drives, especially toward family members, are the main contents that are repressed in the unconscious. A client who lives in an individualistic open culture and who is made aware of her drives is capable, though with difficulty, of coping with these drives and finding direct or indirect ways to express them. This is not so in the case of an Arab/Muslim who is still an integral part of and in the daily control of the family. If the client were to express such forbidden drives, typically she would have to fight a battle which she would have little chance of winning. Many clients cannot deal even with the initial phases of interpreting these drives, prior to any confrontation. Therapists need to bear in mind that the harmony of and loyalty to the family is the basis of the client's trust and security. Discussing negative experiences in the family with a client is threatening enough per se, and may be considered a betrayal, which intensifies the guilt feelings. From my experience I can say that many clients drop out of therapy at this stage; others find the forbidden drives of which they are made newly aware too difficult to handle and their situation is thus exacerbated, not alleviated. As for sexual drives, psychoanalysis considers repressed sexual drives to be the core issue. Again, addressing these issues in a conservative modest society is problematic and may threaten the client, especially if the client and the therapist are of opposite sexes.

In the opening phase of psychodynamic therapy, which typically lasts for several months, the therapist is seen very much as listening passively to what the client expresses. In this phase the client is sometimes placed in ambiguous situations, such as when free association or projective techniques are used. This phase is very confusing for Arab/Muslim clients who are used to being directed and who come to therapy with the expectation of being given concrete advice. This passive role on the side of the therapist may harm the client's trust in the therapist and may cause him to quit therapy.

Cultural barriers render Freudian psychoanalysis unfit for use in the case of the traditional Arab/Muslim client. It may suit a small portion of Arab/Muslim clients who are psychologically individuated and have the power to confront their restricting social environment. Such clients would most likely be educated, Westernized, and males. Nevertheless, psychoanalytic ideas may lead the therapist to suggest some concrete changes in the client's life, without interpreting the rationale behind it and without making the unconscious conscious. For instance, one of my clients, who was too weak to face the anger he felt toward his abusive father, felt better when I directed him to leave his work in his father's carpentry business and transfer to his older uncle's transportation business. This suggestion was presented as a kind of promotion, although it was based on my understanding that the headaches he suffered were associated with a repressed anger toward his father, which he was unable to face. He continued to claim that he loved his father, but felt relief when he could keep his distance from him. This kind of change was acceptable to the father as long as his son continued to work within a family business with the older uncle. This is an example of using the psychoanalytic understanding to make a change without sharing interpretations with the client or making the client's unconscious anger conscious. Similarly, Witztum and Goodman (2003) describe narrative treatments in which they encouraged orthodox religious Jewish clients to act out Jewish rituals. These rituals fit the clients' religious belief system on the one hand, and served some unconscious needs, based on the psychodynamic understanding of the case, on the other. These rituals were effectively used as treatment by encouraging the clients to adhere to their religious or supernatural beliefs, without the therapist having to share any psychodynamic interpretations with the clients that would make the "unconscious conscious."

Alfred Adler's theory (1959) has much merit in relation to Arab/Muslim clients, due to his holistic approach and his heavier emphasis on interpersonal conflicts than on intrapsychic ones. Lifestyle as conceptualized with regard to the self, others, and ideals in simple cognitive terms is very much a practical matter for Arab/Muslim clients. With regard to a culture that discriminates by gender and age, Adler's ideas concerning birth order and sibling jealousy and rivalry may contribute much to the understanding of the dynamics of the Arab/Muslim family. These ideas and Dreikurs' (1949) developments concerning the four goals of children's misbehavior may describe many of the emotional and conduct disorders from which children in Arab/ Muslim families suffer.

Carl Jung's (1953, 1959) idea of the collective unconscious is very relevant to understanding the unconscious dynamic of the Arab/Muslim people. As discussed in Chapter 5, the personality is a collective unit in which vague boundaries are found between the personal mind and the others' minds; the collective unconscious occupies a large amount of space in the personal unconscious. Some other ideas drawn from object-relations theory and other psychodynamic theories, which give priority to social and cultural factors, may be applied to Arabs/Muslims. However, in the application of these ideas the therapist should address repressed needs and drives very cautiously (see Dwairy, 1997b, concerning dealing with the repressed needs).

BEHAVIORAL-COGNITIVE APPROACH

The basic philosophy of behaviorism, which holds that the environment is the prime modifier of people's behavior, fits very well the Arab/Muslim people, who conceptualize themselves as being controlled by external social and supernatural factors. In addition, because this philosophy is concrete, goal oriented, and practical, it also fits the expectations of those clients who do not want to explore intimate topics in any depth. Techniques such as contracts, relaxation, desensitization, and exposure could be applied to Arabs/Muslims to a high degree. All behavior modification techniques could be applied to Arab/Muslim children with the cooperation of parents and teachers. Modeling, which is based on following a social and religious role model, fits the Arab/Muslim culture very well. Parents and teachers may use this technique to influence children's behavior.

The cognitive therapy developed by Albert Ellis (1962) or Aaron Beck (1967/1972), may also be applied, provided that it does not contradict the client's cultural norms and values. Many of the inner thoughts that Ellis might consider irrational may well be rooted in the Arab/Muslim culture. For instance, an inner thought such as "I must always please my family" or "If I disobey my family it will be awful and then I am worthless" would seem irrational to Ellis but is, in fact, very rational in the context of interdependent familial relationships. Encouraging clients to change these inner thoughts may push them toward familial confrontations that they are unable to handle. For any change in the inner thought not to be counterproductive, it must be coordinated with similar changes in the inner thoughts of the familial authority. Cognitive therapy should therefore be conducted within the family framework. Only in parallel with changing the attitudes of the significant members of the family should the therapist encourage the client to change his own inner thoughts. Religious and cultural proverbs may be applied to realize this aim.

In order to persuade parents to be more flexible and moderate in their demands of their children, therapists may remind Muslim clients that when God prohibited alcohol he did so gradually: In the early verses of the Qur'an, God indicated that alcohol is not recommended but is not prohibited (Al-Baqara #219). Only after some years, in later verses, did God strictly prohibit alcohol (Al-Ma'ida #90, 91). Another verse may encourage parents to reduce their pressure on their children, allowing them time to learn and change: *"In Allah la yoghayiro ma beqawmen hatta yoghayirou ma bia'nfosihim"* (Al-Ra'ad #11). [God does not change people until they change themselves.] After using these religious ideas to modify the parents' thoughts, therapists may encourage the young client to step back from the rigid "musts" that dominate her inner thoughts.

Assertiveness training is another behavioral-cognitive technique that is used to encourage people to express themselves without abusing others. Assertive behavior, however, contradicts the *mosayara* value [to please others and get along with them] (Noor El-Deen, 2000), so assertiveness in a society that appreciates *mosayara* is interpreted as rudeness, and its implementation will lead to rejection. This change may be counterproductive for an adolescent if her social environment is not yet ready to understand and accept assertive behavior. In my model of assertiveness training I suggest that the parents and teachers first be prepared before any assertiveness training is implemented with children.

In addition, I suggest offering assertiveness as an option among other options, to allow children who are ready to adopt it to do so, and the others to reject it (Dwairy, 2004a).

HUMANISTIC APPROACH

Humanistic approaches such as Carl Rogers's (1951, 1961), existential ones such as Rollo May's (1950/1977), Fritz Perls's Gestalt therapy (1973/1976), and to some extent the Rational Emotive Behavioral Therapy of Albert Ellis (1962) assume that individuals possess free will and are in control of their own destinies. Most of these approaches give a central role to the self as the entity that runs a person's life. When the "real self" is threatened by conditional regard, rejection, or punishments, a "false self" emerges to cope with social communication. Regardless of how they are intended to achieve it, all humanistic therapies work toward *self-actualization* in order "to make the person be what he really is." Unlike Freud, who assumed that the repressed contents of a person's mind are destructive, sexual, or aggressive, the humanistic approaches believe that the real self is good and constructive, and that the patient can relatively easily be facilitated toward self-actualization.

To return to the collective unindividuated personality of Arabs/Muslims and to the unavoidable interdependence between the individual and the family, one may question the applicability of the "self" theories. Is it right to help a client to free the self in an authoritarian society? In the first place, is therapy even capable of achieving the independence of the client's self within this authoritarian system? Victor Frankl (1946/1959), one of the leading figures in humanistic therapy, may say that a person is always free to choose, even in prison or a concentration camp, but the fact is that the majority of people in authoritarian societies endorse the conformity choice and give up their real selves. This is puzzling: Do they do so based on their free will within this authoritarian system or have they been obliged to make this choice? If they do so freely, what right does the therapist have to interfere? If they were obliged, then how can the therapist face and confront this authoritarian system? In my opinion, psychotherapy cannot and should not compete with culture (see a case study in Dwairy 2002b).

The same reservations which apply to "making the unconscious conscious" and to assertiveness training also apply to achieving a client's self-actualization in an authoritarian collective society. Self-actualization is considered in collective societies as a selfishness that threatens the harmony of the collective, and therefore the client must expect to face rejection and social sanctions, which he is not always able to endure. Often this "solution" may turn into a serious "problem."

Some of the humanistic therapies, such as the person-centered therapy of Carl Rogers, are nondirective and nonjudgmental. The major role of the therapist is to listen, empathize, and reflect her understanding back to the client. This therapy is assumed to help the client feel unconditionally accepted, and is supposed thereby to facilitate growth and self-actualization. Is this also the case for a collective client who came to therapy with the expectation of being given directives and advice? Does this free space provide him with a safe atmosphere or does it rather aggravate his anxiety? My clinical experience and that of many others indicate that nondirective and nonjudgmental therapy is very confusing for Arab/Muslim clients, especially in the early stages of therapy. It does not meet their expectations; they do not know how to use the free space; they become disappointed and dissatisfied with the therapist; and therefore they may quit therapy. Such a nondirective therapy may only be applied to some portion of Arabs/Muslims, typically to those who are educated and tend to be psychologically independent.

The Gestalt therapy of Fritz Perls is also based on the free will and personal responsibility of the client. The therapist attempts to activate the self in direct, active, and confrontational ways, which Arabs/Muslims find unusual, being used to an indirect and "getting along" (*mosayara*) way of communication. Perls's way may therefore be misunderstood and experienced as unbearable criticism or rejection of the client and his culture. In addition, Gestalt therapy and other humanistic therapies focus exclusively on the here-and-now experience. This may seem confusing to Arabs/Muslims who are immersed in their personal and collective history. Avoiding and neglecting the past of an Arab/Muslim client may be experienced as neglecting and rejecting his heritage and culture.

Almost all humanistic principles could be applied to the culture rather than to the person. Unconditional positive regard, listening, and empathy to the cultural component are very important to understanding the Arab/Muslim client. Ivey, Simek-Morgan, D'Andrea, and Ivey (2001) proposed empathy in multicultural counseling in order to see, hear, and feel the world through the client's eyes, ears, and internal world. According to Ivey and his colleagues, the counselor should listen and look, respond using the client's key words and constructs, and then ask: "How does that sound?" Scott and Borodovsky (1990) encourage counselors to make use of the client's expertise and ask the client about his culture. Ridley and Lingle (1996) encourage counselors to play a naive role regarding understanding the client's culture and to avoid automatic interpretations. This attitude does not mean that counselors should ignore their own culture and play a neutral role; but rather that they need to be genuine and aware of their values, and then differentiate these values from those of their clients. By doing so they are more likely to avoid inappropriate value imposition. For Ridley and Lingle, cultural empathy is a multidimensional process that involves cognitive, affective, and communicative understanding and responsiveness. For an Arab/Muslim client that culture constitutes a large portion of the self. Thus cultural acceptance, regard, and empathy is the way to build a therapeutic rapport and help the client find a new order within the Arab/Muslim cultural system.

CULTURE-FREE THERAPY

Some therapists adopt a radical universal approach and disregard cultural differences, claiming that "We all are human beings." This approach is similar to what Sue and Sue (1990) called "color blindness." It seems neutral and universal, but in fact is very much biased toward the individualistic culture in that it gives priority to personal matters over familial and social ones. Saying "we all are human beings" sounds very humane, but it is actually a very humiliating and rejecting thing to hear for a client from a collective background, the essence of whose identity is cultural. As shown in Chapter 5, the personality of an Arab/Muslim constitutes a social collective layer that shares the family's values and norms. For such a client, to exclude culture from the therapeutic encounter is to exclude a significant part of his existence. Instead, therapists are encouraged to show interest and an intention to listen and learn about this layer and to acknowledge the cultural differences, while showing a positive regard for the client's culture. In the treatment of such a client, cultural empathy is very much needed in order to establish rapport and gain deep understanding.

SYSTEMIC ECLECTICISM, MULTICULTURAL COUNSELING AND THERAPY, AND MULTIMODAL THERAPY

The way different approaches of psychotherapy have dealt with people is very similar to the old story about how a group of blind people dealt with an elephant they encountered. The one who touched the elephant's leg described the elephant as a pillar; the one who touched his trunk described the animal as a big pipe; the one who touched the tail, as a rope; the one who touched the ear, as a carpet; and so on. All were right and described real, though different, experiences with the elephant, but none of them described the whole elephant. Sue and Sue (1990) postulated that "each school of counseling has its strength, but they may be one-dimensional; they concentrate only on feelings, or only on cognitions, or only on behaviors. We need to realize that we are *feeling, thinking, behaving, social, cultural* and *political* beings" (p. 73). They proposed adopting a systemic eclecticism rather than being random, haphazard, and inconsistent in using counseling strategies.

Multicultural counseling and therapy (MCT) (see chaps. 5–6 in Ivey, Ivey, & Simek-Morgan, 1997) is also useful to Arabs/Muslims. It is a metatheoretical approach that recognizes that all counseling approaches exist within a cultural context, and serves as a framework that integrates these approaches in counseling. MCT recognizes the utility of Western theories and recommends making changes in the way counseling is conducted based on the understanding of the individual within her cultural context.

Dogmatic therapy, which conceptualizes the client's experience according to a certain theory, such as a psychodynamic, behavioral, cognitive, or "self" theory, typically neglects much of the client's experience. This kind of work may serve the theory much more than the client. The multimodal therapy proposed by Arnold Lazarus (2000) suggests another good solution for the use of the various therapies. It is a comprehensive, systemic therapy that employs every strategy to intervene in seven modalities: Behavior, Affect, Sensation, Imagery, Cognition, Interpersonal, and Drugs/Biological (BASIC ID). Lazarus suggests blending diverse theories harmoniously into a congruent framework and adapting the therapeutic package to each client. Through flexibility and technical eclecticism therapists may use procedures drawn from different sources, without necessarily subscribing to the theories or disciplines that spawned them (Lazarus, 2000). Despite the fact that BASIC ID does not address social and cultural domains, it allows enough flexibility to suit clients from different cultures. *Bridging,* according to Lazarus, refers to a procedure in which the therapist deliberately adopts the client's preferred modality. If a client is preoccupied with somatic complaints, the therapist may listen to and intervene in this domain through relaxation exercises or drugs. And if the client is imaginative or metaphoric in her descriptions, the therapist may utilize imagery and metaphors. Hence, Lazarus' approach enables the use of various therapies within a culturally sensitive framework.

For many non-Western clients, psychotherapy in a clinical setting seems alien, and orientation to therapy and outreach therapy is therefore recommended (Sue & Sue, 1990). Since psychotherapy is not a common experience for Arabs/Muslims, orientation to therapy in the initial stages is recommended in order to modify expectations and to help the client take her own share of responsibility during therapy. In the case of some traditional clients, for whom the clinic setting may be too alien, the therapist may consider outreach therapy in order to meet them in their normal setting such as homes or mosques. Therapists can thus express in action their respect and acceptance of the client's cultural background. In addition, this visit to the client's environment may provide invaluable information about the social and cultural background.

SUMMARY

Therapists who work with Arabs/Muslims may learn and adopt many strategies and techniques from Western theories of psychotherapy. This adoption should be based on a culturally sensitive approach in order to fit the intervention to the client and avoid counterproductive results, such as the generation of new unresolvable conflicts with the family and society. Psychoanalytic interpretation that reveals unconscious contents may be productive only for a small portion of Arabs/Muslims, who are closer to the Western culture; otherwise, the therapist may give practical advice based on psychoanalytic understanding, without revealing the unconscious. The humanistic approach is very useful when applied to the culture rather than to the self. A nondirective relationship or encouraging self-actualization may be counterproductive in clients from a collective society. The behavioral approach is very much suited to Arabs/Muslims. Cognitive therapy should be based on cultural norms and values. A comprehensive systemic blending of many approaches, which is suggested by the Systemic Eclecticism, MCT, and the multimodal therapy, is recommended.

Chapter 9

Toward Culturally Sensitive Counseling and Psychotherapy

Psychotherapy is actually an encounter between at least two cultures: the one (or more) to which the client belongs and another one (or more) to which the therapist belongs. Besides the original social culture of the therapist, his or her psychotherapeutic approaches constitute a sort of culture too. They include norms, values, and rituals that are part of the general individualistic culture. Intake interview, private conversation, and weekly meetings are some of the norms. Within this culture self-actualization, reality testing, objectivity, and reasoning are of great value, while repression, oppression, hallucination, imagination, and spirituality as a way of life are not appreciated. Each approach directs the therapist how to progress stage by stage in therapy, sometimes in a ritualistic fashion, to achieve the needed change.

Cultural transference and countertransference take place in this encounter. Each side judges the other through his or her own cultural lens. Western and individualistic therapists may consider the collective personality as immature, and therefore intervene to facilitate independence; they may consider the husbands' and fathers' control of wives and children as abuse, and therefore conduct counseling and legal actions intended to stop this abuse. On the other hand, a culturally collective client may misjudge the attempts of a psychodynamic therapist to understand sexual and other intimate experiences, and consider such interference rude or malignant. Nondirective therapy may be considered by the client as a sort of indifference toward his suffering. Within this cultural encounter, which side is expected to be empathic toward the other? Understanding and handling of cultural transference and countertransference is solely the responsibility of the counselor. She is responsible for being aware of her cultural package and must avoid judging the client from a cultural perspective; at the same time she is responsible for attempting to listen, understand, and be culturally empathic. In this encounter it is the counselor who ought to join and identify with the client's culture and work within it. As mentioned in the preceding chapter, a judgmental attitude toward the culture is unethical and counterproductive. It is recommended that the Rogerian unconditional positive regard be applied in relation to clients' culture. Therapists should ask questions, such as "How is this usually carried out in your culture?" "How does your family perceive this action?" "What made your parents upset?" "What is it about that that makes you feel shy?" "Explain this to me," "help me understand," and "tell me more." Paraphrasing and reflecting back to the client what the therapist has understood about the culture may help the therapist avoid misunderstanding.

THERAPY IS NOT THE PLACE FOR CHANGING CULTURE

Many counselors and therapists who face cultural differences find it unethical not to facilitate or educate their clients, especially female clients, toward their rights to freedom and equality, and not to use their authority to control or punish male hegemony. Such an attitude, in fact, constitutes a confrontation with the clients' culture, and therefore it is itself unethical and useless, if not harmful, for the following three reasons.

Culture has its own rationale that is based on collective experience and wisdom. Cultural actions take their legitimacy from the collective experience of the people. For instance, the central role of the mother and the marginal role of the father in the African American family have their roots in slavery. The male slaves were exploited and controlled by their owners, and kept at a distance from their families, leaving the females to "rule the roost." In this case to blame the fathers is to blame the victim. On the other hand, victims like these fathers also need help to liberate themselves from the abuse and trauma. They first need to be understood and be empathized with in order to be able to change their lives; they need empathic therapy like any other traumatized people. By the same token, the punishment meted out by Arab/Muslim fathers to their children should be understood, though not justified, within the cultural context. As a collective society, the family or tribe is the unit to which all individuals are expected to adhere in order to maintain its harmony and functioning. Any individual behavior that threatens this harmony is punishable. This controlling relationship is very similar to the relationship between the modern state and its citizens. A state does everything in its power to protect the security and harmony within it and punishes any citizen who disobeys the laws or betrays the state. State laws in an individualistic society are not necessarily more humane than social norms in a collective one, and the state punishments are no more legitimate than the punishment meted out by the family authority in a collective society. In the last analysis, both state laws and cultural norms are expressions of the collective will. Therapists do not have the right to judge cultural practices as good or bad, but should rather judge them according to whether they are functional or dysfunctional from the point of view of the client. They should try to exploit the culture for the sake of therapy.

Confronting the culture can harm the client. Clients tend to be the weakest party in the social system, and therefore it is unethical to make them serve as the champions of change. Applying pressure on a client to "be himself," encouraging an adolescent girl to fulfill her right of choice, or an Arab/Muslim wife to disobey her authoritarian husband may lead to a tough confrontation with a rigid cultural authority that may end in unbearable results for the client, such as neglect, physical punishment, or divorce. Some therapists may say that these results are still better than allowing the cultural system in question to continue. I say: Ask your clients if this is what they want. If you really want to facilitate their independence, do not decide for them. Do not be sure that an Arab/Muslim wife prefers divorce to living within this cultural system. Before going ahead toward confrontation with the culture, therapists and counselors should make sure that the client wants it, is able to endure it, and is prepared for the results.

Of course, counselors and therapists do have a major role in mobilizing social and cultural change, but the clinic is not the field for this change. The clinic is the arena in which the change necessary to make the client feel better is achieved. The arenas in which counselors and therapists ought to work to mobilize social change are lectures, articles, social organizations, and lobbying. In these arenas they play their part as citizens, may be committed to their own values, and are allowed to be revolutionary. In the clinic they play their part as therapists who are committed to their mandate to help the client.

Confrontation with the culture is a lost battle and it may cause the client to quit therapy. In the encounter between therapist and culture, therapists should realize their limited power and avoid overstepping the mark. In my clinical experience I have seen many families who quit therapy when either the culture or the familial authority was slightly challenged or even when the family felt misunderstood or experienced a cultural gap. Typically, it is the familial figure of authority, to whom the client submits unconditionally, who is responsible for the departure from therapy. In some cases, when the client has revealed negative feelings toward the family in a private therapeutic conversation, acute distress symptoms may appear that would cause her to quit therapy. In a case study of an Arabic woman (Dwairy, 2002b), I described the dynamic of a "lost battle" between the therapeutic tools that a therapist wields and the power of the culture. During this therapy, a young Arab/Muslim woman, who had suffered demanding and abusive treatment since her childhood and after her marriage, consistently joined forces with the abusive husband and family against any therapeutic change, until finally they quit therapy. Fortunately, the same abusive culture upgraded her status in the family after she had borne a male child. For the aforementioned reasons, the therapist should work within the client's culture through facilitating new coalitions and employing ideas and factors from within the culture to help the client.

FITTING THERAPY TO EACH CLIENT

As explained in previous chapters, Arabs/Muslims are very culturally diverse and they are spread along a continuum of individuation. Some are Westernized and possess an independent identity and self that is differentiated from their families', while others are very traditional and possess a collective identity and self. The majority fall in the collective or the bicultural range, having two layers to their personality: a social layer and a private layer (see Chapter 5). Of course, therapists who work with Arab/Muslim immigrants in the United States may encounter some clients who do possess an independent identity. Given this diversity, there is no single therapeutic method that fits all Arab/Muslim clients, and the therapist should tailor the therapeutic package to the cultural characteristics of the client.

On the other hand, one needs to bear in mind that Western therapies are not uniform, but rather vary along a continuum of the depth to which the unconscious is explored. Some, such as psychoanalysis, dig deep into the unconscious and aim to make unconscious drives conscious. At the opposite pole, there are others that work on the behavioral or symptomatic level, such as behavioral therapy or psychiatric treatments. Between the two poles there are many psychotherapies that vary in their approaches toward unconscious dynamics. The humanistic approach deals very gently with unconscious contents without pushing or imposing interpretations. Cognitive therapy deals with unconscious inner thoughts in order to change them to conscious rational ones. Gestalt therapy addresses unconscious contents in the here-and-now context, without dealing directly with childhood and client-family relationships.

To tailor the therapy to the client, the therapist may match the cultural continuum of the client with the therapeutic continuum.

Cultural continuum:

Individuated ID -- Collective ID

Therapeutic continuum:

Psychoanalysis -- Behavioral Therapy

Generally speaking, the more individuated the client and the more she possesses an independent identity, the more likely she is to be helped by a variety of Western therapies, including psychoanalysis.

To be more precise, three psychocultural factors of the client should be considered when making the match: level of individuation, strictness of the family, and ego strength.

1. Individuation. Individuation reflects the proportion of the client's personality that the collective social layer occupies. The more the values, attitudes, and belief system of the client are differentiated from his family's, the more the client is individuated. Individuated clients are those who feel free to adopt attitudes that are similar to or different from the attitudes of their families without feeling threatened or guilty. Such clients may fit psychodynamic therapy because they are able to acknowledge and face unconscious negative feelings toward family members or their own forbidden needs during therapy. Generally speaking, Arabs/Muslims who were exposed to Western culture during their education or as a result of immigration tend to be more individuated. This is a general rule that should be validated in each case, since some of the immigrants may defensively retreat from the Western culture to find refuge in a more fanatic adherence to the collective/authoritarian values and norms.

2. Strictness of the Family. Once a client becomes aware of negative feelings or needs, she may need to express them in the familial context, which naturally may provoke oppressive responses. If the family is too traditional and strict and reacts in an extremely punishing way, this may abort any therapeutic change and cause a therapeutic regression. Therefore, therapists should make sure that the family is ready to absorb the client's expression of feelings before bringing negative or forbidden needs and feelings to the client's consciousness. They need to work with the family to prepare her to absorb the changes. The level of strictness of the Arab/Muslim family very much depends on the client's gender and on the content of the revealed drives. Typically, families are stricter toward females than males concerning sexual behavior and need for more freedom.

3. Client's Ego Strength. The family strictness influences the client, in proportion to his ability to cope with and endure their responses. Moderate strictness may influence a "fragile" client in a different way from another client, who has the ability to prevail and cope with the oppression or punishment of the family. Emotional stability, self-control, self-esteem, and reality testing are some factors that are associated with ego strength. Individuation, too, is associated with ego strength. Individuated clients are supposed to be able to endure the rejection and punishment of the family on their own.

Clients who are individuated and have enough strength to endure the family rejection and punishment are able to undergo psychotherapy that digs deep into the unconscious and reveals negative and forbidden contents. Otherwise, therapists should avoid this kind of therapy and try to help the client through behavioral therapy or other psychiatric or indirect therapies that will be discussed in Chapter 11. The idea of avoiding insights that may be troublesome for the client has been emphasized by other therapists who work with collective communities. In their 1997 article titled "Value-Sensitive Therapy: Learning from Ultra-Orthodox Patients," Heilman and Witztum asserted that therapists must pursue "a therapeutic strategy that is sensitive to the patients' values, even when this seems to oppose commonly accepted therapeutic approaches" (p. 523). They suggest considering the benefit of the client before interpreting unconscious drives. As an example, they presented the case of a rabbi who experienced sexual impotence at age 52. Based on their evaluation, they concluded that the rabbi had a repressed homosexual drive. They believed that his impotence was a sort of defensive inhibition of the libido in order to avoid the threat of consciously experiencing homosexual feelings. These drives were completely rejected according to the rabbinical value system. When these drives were hinted at in therapy, the rabbi said that he would rather kill himself, if he really had such desires. The dilemma of the therapist was whether to "reveal to the rabbi his apparent homosexual or bisexual nature or . . . help the rabbi suppress that nature or sublimate it so that he can continue to live in the sexually regulated and highly structured *haredi* world" (p. 535). Based on a value-sensitive approach the therapist decided to deal with the symptoms of impotence with medication and relaxation techniques and intentionally avoided giving "a psychodynamic interpretation of the symptoms that would allow the rabbi to face the underlying issues of his sexuality" (p. 535).

In order to fit therapy to client correctly, these three factors—level of individuation, strictness of the family, and ego strength—should be among those targets assessed before therapy begins. Unconventional diagnostic tools are needed, such as Talking About a Significant Object (Dwairy, 2001, 2003) or the Berg-Cross and Chinen (1995) intake interview mentioned in Chapter 6, to achieve this goal.

CULTURANALYSIS: A WITHIN-CULTURE THERAPY

As mentioned before, therapy is not a tool with which to change the client's culture. Culture should rather be exploited to bring about therapeutic change. The therapist should identify subtle contradictions within the belief system of the client and employ cultural aspects that may facilitate change. Just as a *psychoanalyst* analyses the psychological domain and brings conflicting aspects to the consciousness (e.g., aggression and guilt) in order to mobilize change, so a *culturanalyst* analyses the client's belief system and brings contradicting aspects to the consciousness in order to mobilize revision in attitudes and behavior. The assumption that underlies *culturanalysis* is that culture influences people's lives unconsciously. When therapists inquire into and learn about the client's culture, they may find some unconscious aspects that are in conflict with the conscious attitudes of the client. Once the therapist brings these aspects to the awareness of the client, a significant change may be effected. Unlike the unconscious drives that are revealed through psychoanalysis, these intraculture conflicts are not supposed to be threatening because all aspects revealed are culturally and morally legitimized.

This process can be described in humanistic terms too. In much the same way that a Rogerian therapist establishes an unconditional positive regard and empathy to facilitate the coming forward of the real authentic self, a culturanalyst establishes positive regard and empathy to the culture and facilitates the coming forward of more and more aspects of the culture that were denied and that may be employed to effect change. Alternatively, one can understand this process in terms of generating cognitive dissonance within the client's belief system that necessitates change.

Regardless of the theoretical explanation, in order to conduct a "within-culture therapy," therapists need to be open and incorporate several aspects of the culture in the therapy in order to create a new dynamic within the client's culture. Beside empathy, a thorough inquiry into the client's culture in order to identify the cultural aspects that may be employed in therapy is needed. Here are some examples of within-culture therapy.

Samer: Working Within a Client's Belief System

Samer, who was 22 years old, suffered from a depressive mood, negative self-concept, and pessimistic attitude. Since his parents' divorce when he was 5 years old, he had suffered from emotional neglect at home, and from emotional abuse of some abusive peers at school. His past experience explained his negative self-concept and his pessimism. My assessment revealed that he had a low level of individuation, his extended family with whom he lived and worked was very traditional, religious, and strict, and his ego strength was low. Based on these facts, I avoided revealing any negative feelings or forbidden needs to preclude his feeling guilty, and instead encouraged him to talk about his beliefs and values.

It was clear that his was an almost completely Islamic religious point of view. He explained any negative event that happened to him as a punishment from God for not praying five times a day. In fact these negative events—a minor car crash, breaking up with a friend, and missing the bus on his way home—frequently happen to many people. He was convinced that God was not satisfied with him and that therefore God was punishing him with these events. Samer's way of avoiding these "punishments" was to adhere more and more to religion. He came angry and despairing in one session because of a couple of minor negative events, such as that his request for an upgrade of his salary had been denied. He was angry because he did his best to adhere to all religious duties and avoid anything that might dissatisfy God. "What more could I do?" he said desperately.

After I expressed understanding and empathy, I told him that maybe he does pray five times a day, but maybe he does not appreciate the grace of God enough. I said, "You are employed while many others are unemployed, you are healthy and handsome while many others are ill and unattractive, you have enough money to spend on entertainment with your friends, and you have many good friends and a family that has already built a house for you to live in after your marriage. Instead of appreciating all these good things that God gave you, you became angry and blamed Him because your request for a salary upgrade was denied. I think the basic requirement of religion is to appreciate the grace of God. This appreciation is the essence of believing in God, so your prayers may not seem authentic to Him, if you do not really see and feel and celebrate what God has given you. Do you appreciate the grace of God?" I asked. This confused him and made him realize that his pessimism in fact contradicted the requirement to celebrate God's grace. My words led him to start thinking positively and to recognize the many positive things in his life and put the negative events in the right proportion.

I gave him a task for the next session: to add to his formal praying authentic thanks to God for His grace. This task was aimed at making him aware, during the following week, of some components of the religious belief that he had been neglecting. We continued to work on appreciating the grace of God during the therapeutic sessions. Gradually a significant change started to occur in his depression.

Because my words were drawn from his religious belief system, they were more effective in changing Samer's way of thinking than any cognitive intervention that Albert Ellis or Aaron Beck could have suggested to eradicate irrational or dysfunctional thoughts. Regular cognitive therapy would have contradicted his religious belief system. For instance, suggesting to him that he should think positively and widen his perspective to see the positive things in his life would seem alien and unconvincing to him, and might have contradicted his belief in his need to adhere completely to God. This might have caused him to reject and avoid positive thoughts about himself. In fact, within his religious belief system there was no way of disputing his irrational thinking in a rational framework.

Matta: Avoiding Destructive Confrontation

Matta, a young child from a religious Christian Arab family, suffered from a variety of anxiety symptoms such as obsessions and compulsions. His mother was very demanding and restrictive. She expected him to fill the role that her neglecting and almost absent husband did not. She worked as a teller in a bank and wanted her son to help her in the household and to take care of his younger 2-year-old brother. They came to me first when Matta was 5 years old and had suffered a week of acute anxiety. The anxiety had started when the boy was playing at making flying models and paper rockets and launching them. During this game a rocket had hit the portrait of the Virgin Mary that hung on the guest room wall. He became anxious and repeatedly prayed to Mary to forgive him. According to psychoanalysis this anxiety may be understood as a result of acting out a symbolic aggression toward a mother symbol—Mary. For unknown reasons, the mother and son never returned after the first session.

After several years, at approximately age 10, Matta was referred to me again after he had developed leukemia. At this stage his anxiety was severe and he had developed obsessive thoughts and compulsive rituals. The obsessive thoughts were associated with aggressive actions toward the mother. He also heard a voice in his head telling him to disobey his mother. Sometimes this voice ordered him to kill her. Every time this voice was heard, Matta became anxious and started ritualistic praying, asking for forgiveness and for the voice to be taken away. In the last month before he came to the clinic, he had become preoccupied with praying almost all day.

Before he was referred to me the second time, a Jewish psychologist, obviously a psychoanalyst, had interpreted the voice for him and told him that the voice was in fact expressing denied negative feelings and wishes toward his mother. This interpretation aggravated his anxiety and its symptoms, so that he refused to leave his mother's side and became afraid of losing her. He multiplied his ritualistic praying to prove to God that he was a good boy who loved his mother. When he was referred to me at this stage I focused on his good behavior and said I was impressed with his care of his mother. I directed his mother to acknowledge this care in her behavior and in words such as "you are a good boy, I am lucky to have a son like you." I told him that I believed that the Jewish therapist did not know the truth about how much he cared for and loved his mother.

In the second meeting we talked about the voice. I told him that "this voice," too, did not really know him and that it was surely wrong and misinterpreted his feelings. This attitude had a very calming effect on him. We continued to talk about his anxiety after hearing the voice and about his need to make sure that God would not believe the voice, but know that he was a good boy. I asked him: "Do you really believe that almighty God believes this voice? Do you think that God really needs you to tell Him a thousand times a day that you are a good boy?" The conversation centered on these questions made Matta realize that he was not treating God as an almighty power who knows everything, but rather as an ignorant entity that could be misled by a dumb voice. I directed him to pray every morning and tell God that he acknowledges His ability to know the truth. This realization allowed him to disregard and deny the voice, and gradually to quit the ritualistic prayers. After a couple of weeks the voice ceased.

In the following meetings, I focused on his feelings about his mother's demands. He expressed feelings of distress toward her. I talked about these feelings and emphasized that they were far from being anything to do with hurting her, and that these feelings of distress did not negate or reduce his real love and care for her. Within a dyadic work with Matta and his mother I facilitated him to express distress and anger toward his mother at a bearable level. Within this context, I continued working with both of them, and his anxiety and compulsions completely faded away.

Obviously, many contradictions existed within this case. Of course, Matta's aggressive feelings, on the one hand, and his love, dependence, and conscience, on the other, constituted a major contradiction or conflict. Instead of initiating a confrontation with these feelings that he seemed unable to endure, I exploited another contradiction within his belief system, the one between his religious rituals on the one hand and his belief that almighty God knows the truth on the other. This confrontation brought him to realize that the rituals were not functional, and that he should rely on God's ability to know the truth.

JOINING THE FAMILIAL AUTHORITY

In the case of an Arab/Muslim family it is easy to identify an oppressive or abusive attitude toward the client, especially when the client is a girl or a wife. For a Western therapist it is very tempting to go ahead and confront and control that authority. As I mentioned before, this confrontation may not help the client, may be counterproductive, and may cause the client to quit therapy. Fisek and Kagitcibasi (1999) emphasized the importance of identifying and understanding the hierarchy of the family and of the therapist-client relationship. They suggested promoting togetherness rather than promoting false equality within Turkish families.

It is recommended that therapists adopt an accepting and respectful attitude toward the familial authority, unite with it in order to detect its positive aspects, and use it to facilitate therapeutic change. In the first session with authoritarian fathers or husbands, I would say that I really appreciated their unique attitude and readiness, and the effort involved in coming with the client to therapy to get help, despite the stigma and the expense. This is the first step of openly identifying with some positive aspect within the familial authority. I would then emphasize my need for his help during the therapy, explaining that I needed to learn from him about the case, the family, and his thoughts concerning the solution. I emphasized that I needed him because "only he" could make a change in the client's life.

Not infrequently have I discovered that the oppressive father might have a lot of love, care, concern, and anxiety for his children. By identifying with these aspects, the therapist may empower him and make his feelings more explicit in his attitude and behavior. Instead of adopting a judgmental attitude to the oppression, the therapist may ask the father to explain what made him do something. "What were you afraid would happen, if you did not do that?" Such questions help the father talk about his care and anxiety. It makes him feel that he is understood and to want to cooperate and get help. In many cases the oppressing father or husband is afraid of the attitude of others in the community and needs help dealing with these anxieties.

To convince a father or husband to revise his abusive attitude, therapists may employ religious and cultural references. Therapists may refer clients to a religious authority that gives legitimacy to a new attitude. In one of the cases, I referred a father to a sheikh for advice concerning his daughter, who wished to study in college. The sheikh mentioned to him that the Prophet encouraged girls to learn. This gave the father the support and legitimacy to face anyone who might blame him because he allowed his daughter to study outside the village.

In the Qur'an there are many verses that may be employed by therapists to facilitate change. To a neglecting or abusive parent, a therapist may quote the verse, "*Al-mal wa al-banoon zenato al-hayat al-dunya*" (Al-Kahf #46) [Wealth and children are the ornament of life on earth]. To encourage clients to control rage, therapists may quote many verses such as: "*Wajannaten ardoha assamawat wa al-ʿard wueʿidat lilmutaqeen. Allatheen . . . walkathemeen al ghayth wal ʿafeen al-nas*" (Al-ʿUmran #133, 134) [A heaven as wide as the sky and earth is prepared for believers. Those who . . . control their rage and forgive people.] To encourage dialogue in a family or to persuade stubborn clients to listen, therapists may mention the Islamic principle of getting advice, *shura* (Shura #38). This principle suggests a democratic advisory technique for making decisions on controversial issues. To alleviate guilt feelings, Islam may suggest fulfilling the zakah fundamental of Islam (to provide financial help to the poor). All these verses and proverbs and many others may be employed in therapy, either as the advice that Arab/Muslim clients typically request or as a reframing that provides new meanings or as new inner thoughts within a cognitive therapy. Therapists are not, of course, expected to know these verses, and may therefore be supervised by sheikhs or other religious or cultural leaders concerning specific issues that arise in therapy. They may refer the client to a religious leader for advice.

EMPLOYING THE FAMILY TO DEAL WITH SEXUAL ABUSE

Physical abuse or incest cases are among the toughest dilemmas in a collective family that lives in a Western country. When an abused wife or girl approaches the state institutions and asks for help against an abuser from the family, her community will consider her a traitor who threatens the family reputation. The whole family therefore becomes defensive, and typically all its members are enlisted against the state law and against the victim. Within this context, enforcing state law may turn the abuser into a victim in the eyes of his community, on the one hand, and revictimize the original victim, on the other. In many cases it leads to divorce before the wife is ready for it. In the case of child abuse or incest, enforcing state laws may cause the victim to be rejected in an extreme way and to be subtly punished by the family.

Generally speaking, the goals of state laws are to protect the victim, to punish the abuser, and to provide help and therapy to the victim and the family. Assuming that the function of the family (or tribe) in a collective society is parallel to the function of the state in an individualistic one, then counselors may attempt to employ the familial authority to achieve these same goals within the family. Abu-Baker and Dwairy (2003) suggest a practical model of intervention that employs the familial authority to protect the victim and punish the abuser, and facilitates therapy. The state law according to this model is the last refuge and may be used as a mobilizer that pressurizes the family to take responsibility in order to avoid enforcing the state laws, and thereby saves the face of the family. According to this model, counselors and state officers should work together to persuade the family to cooperate in order to achieve the law's objectives. Within the framework of this cooperation, the family is capable of protecting the victim and punishing the perpetrator. The rejection of the family in a collective culture is one of the harshest punishments. In addition, the family is capable of physically expelling the perpetrator from the family while it takes care of his nuclear family, and of denying the perpetrator's rights in the family property and inheritance. According to Abu-Baker and Dwairy's model, in co-operation with counselors and state officers the family arranges a meeting for all family members including the victim and the perpetrator. During this meeting the family leadership "publicly" condemns the abuse and the abuser, expresses its support for the victim, and makes the perpetrator apologize "publicly" to the victim. This act has proven to be very powerful in deterring the perpetrator and in empowering the victim and other potential victims.

SUMMARY

In this chapter it is recommended that counselors and therapists who work with Arab/Muslim immigrants tailor therapy to the individuation level and ego strength of the clients, and to the traditionalism and strictness of the family. In the case of clients who are culturally collective, it is recommended that therapists avoid confrontation with culture or with the familial authority; rather, they need to work within the client's cultural frame of reference and employ factors within the client and within the family to achieve the therapeutic change.

Chapter 10

Family Therapy with Arab/Muslim Women

KHAWLA ABU-BAKER

The manner in which Arab women start therapy and terminate it reflects their status in their family, their psychological stress, and the opportunities available to them for transforming their situation. It is known that Arab women seek mental health therapy more than do Arab men (Abu-Baker, 2003). They arrive at therapy seeking help for the same mental health problems from which women in other societies suffer. However, unlike women in other societies, very few Arab women can decide for themselves the length of their therapy or the changes they would consider making in their lives as a result of therapy. The main factors involved in this regard are the restrictions on Arab women's freedom to use money and their freedom of mobility outside their residential areas. These factors are among the main problems of which these women complain as a source of stress in their lives.

For example, Janan, a teacher in her early thirties, was married to a failed businessman who for many years had kept the family deeply in debt. He controlled Janan's salary and decision-making capacities. As a result of his controlling personality, Janan lived as a victim of psychological violence for many years. When she decided to start therapy, she was in a very stressed state. However, when the husband learned about her need for therapy, he forced her to stop, claiming that she could not afford it financially. Janan kept coming to therapy for five more sessions without her husband's knowledge. This "secret" aggravated her psychological condition, since she was afraid that her husband would declare her to be a disobedient wife. Janan decided to terminate therapy. Her main problem was that in the course of her marriage she had been forced to lose her own voice and to learn to behave as an obedient wife to an abusive and malfunctioning husband. Therapy had to help Janan maintain her self-respect and at the same time a sense of constancy and devoted loyalty to her family.

In another case, Siham, a depressed uneducated housewife, called the clinic repeatedly for about a year, seeking telephone therapy. When she learned that she had to come to the clinic, it took her 6 more months to convince her husband to drive her to the clinic. Siham, who had no direct access to money and did not have a driving license, was not, in accordance with local traditions, allowed to leave her village unless accompanied by a male relative. Nevertheless, she made every effort to convince her husband to bring her to the clinic twice. When the husband learned that therapy would require a longer time and more expense, he announced: "I have no time or money for this. Let her parents take care of her." Siham was afraid to be labeled "crazy," a legitimate religious and social reason for divorcing an Arab wife. She asked to terminate therapy immediately.

CULTURAL INFLUENCE OF GENDER ON THERAPY

Such cases constantly remind the therapist who works with Arab women of the male supremacy in the Arab society. Although Arab societies and Arab families vary in each Arab country in terms of the process and practice of traditionalism, religiosity, modernization, and Westernization (Abu-Baker, in press-a; Joseph, 1999, 2000), the frame of reference of the society is still male dominance. Cainkar (1996) described Arab society, both Christian and Muslim, as socially stratified among classes. Arabs are very religious, patriarchal, and patrilineal, and place a high value on family ties. They believe that men and women were created for different, but complementary, roles. Arabs in the Middle East and in the United States have double standards regarding men and women. Women should be watched and controlled, while men enjoy privileges, such as having more rights, being served all their lives by females, and being recognized socially and culturally as superior to women.

The truth is that it is very difficult to judge Arab society as a whole. Rather, each aspect should be studied within its context. The same couple may be judged as Westernized or modern according to some aspects, and very traditional according to others. There is no one yardstick by which to judge an individual's behavior in Arab families, a situation which makes the work of therapists that much more challenging. In all therapy cases, both therapist and client have to discuss the reasons, processes, and dynamics behind adopting social values and norms. The role of the therapist here is *anthrotherapist*: a person who is very well acquainted with the social structure and uses that knowledge to mediate between the social and the mental health context.

Suraya, a 24-year-old teacher, came to couples therapy after 2 years of constant arguments with her husband, Tawfiq, a 28-year-old bank employee. Tawfiq's mother, who lived on the first floor of the same building as the couple, had demanded that Suraya, who is her first daughter-in-law, help her in her household duties, as expected in traditional families. Tawfiq, thinking that this was a problem between women, decided not to interfere. Suraya was collapsing under the heavy duties she had to shoulder between her job as a teacher, and her responsibilities as housekeeper of her own house and assistant to her mother-in-law. The situation was exacerbated when Suraya gave birth to twins, a year after her marriage. In therapy Suraya complained that during her 3 years of married life she had moved from being the indulged, spoiled elder daughter of her family of origin to being a fatigued, burnt-out wife and mother. Tawfiq, who adhered in his marriage to the same type of schedule as he had when single, reacted to Suraya's complaint with the statement, "This is what all wives do." It was very difficult for Tawfiq to empathize with Suraya's complaints. He had been the first in his generation in his extended family to marry a woman who worked outside her home and earned money. All his younger sisters and the other women in his family were housewives who did the same type of jobs inside their extended families as were required of Suraya.

Rural women in the Middle East have always worked in the family fields; however, they were not recognized as a labor force, since they were never paid. Although Arab societies, especially urban ones, expect Arab women to contribute to the family income, they have not yet internalized the concept of men contributing to the household and child rearing duties (Abu-Baker, 2003). The challenge that gave Tawfiq insight was a week of thinking about a "productive way to solve the marital problem." He had to consider whether he would like to use the Islamic and traditional norms, which force men to be the sole person responsible for providing the family needs, and thus free Suraya from her work outside so that she could focus on her traditional duties. Tawfiq, a bank officer, learned during the week the real meaning of the contribution of Suraya's salary to the well-being of the family. On that basis, he became empathic with her complaints and was ready to support changes in her situation. Tawfiq devoted more time to taking care of the twins, helped prepare the food, and asked his mother to help Suraya as a working woman and stop demanding her help upon her arrival home. Without the support and understanding of Tawfiq, the only other option open to Suraya to change her situation was a continuous frontal struggle with her husband and in-laws, mostly without any social or psychological support from her family of origin or friends.

When the therapist is female and the clients are female, it is essential to voice the unbiased, gendered stance and nonjudgmental ideology to which the therapist holds. For example, feminist therapists should not force their female clients to observe their own marital lives from the point of view of feminism. The same is also true for ultraorthodox Muslim or Christian therapists. In some cases, men relate to the therapist as a handyman whom they expect to "fix" their wives for them according to their needs. Highly professional behavior is the best way for the therapist to deal with such situations. Despite the gender inequality, Arab society treats therapists as professionals and takes their instructions seriously (Al-Issa, 1989, 1995; Okasha, 1993).

In summary, in most cases of therapy with Arab women, it is crucial to find ways to interest the men related to the woman in the therapy process in order to guarantee the support of the woman's environment in changing her life conditions and to preclude a premature termination of the therapy process.

ARAB/MUSLIM WOMEN'S ISSUES IN THERAPY

When men come to a female therapist for individual therapy, their choice represents a declaration of their belief in the therapist's professional skills. In contrast to female clients in therapy, male clients are free to decide when, how long, to what depth, and on which aspects of their lives they would like to work in therapy. They do not fear being labeled crazy, nor can they be forced to terminate therapy under any circumstances. Additionally, they are able to make more independent decisions regarding their private lives than women can. In cases when there is no hope of repairing the marriage, if the husband is the party who is convinced that the marriage must be terminated, the process of arranging the necessary changes in the family's life will be very fast, including the divorce. In cases when it is the wife who demands an end to the marriage, the therapist has to deal with the husband's resistance as well as the additional stress for the wife caused by the efforts of the extended families on both sides to convince her that she has made the wrong decision. An example of two different couples who started therapy at the same time will illustrate this point.

In the first case, the couple had been married for 4 years and had two children. The husband said that he had realized in the first year of marriage that his decision to marry his wife had been wrong, but he gave the marriage another chance, and they had one more child. Now he came to therapy for help in terminating the marriage without causing extra damage to himself, the wife, or the children. Two weeks after that session the husband arranged to leave the marriage, the house, and the village. He paid for his wife's therapy to learn how to deal with the social stress experienced by divorced women, although he never listened to complaints about the social stress suffered by their extended families. He was convinced that he had the freedom to decide.

In the second case, the wife had been convinced that she did not want her husband a month after the arranged marriage. Her family convinced her that she would ruin her reputation if she insisted on getting a divorce after only a month of marriage. Nine years later, with two unwanted children, she came to marriage therapy, forced by her husband because she insisted on getting a divorce. He believed that therapy would "fix" her thoughts. Over the years, the wife developed an abiding hatred for her husband and was not able to agree to any type of compromise or second chance in her marriage. She secretly had had an extra-marital relationship and convinced herself that it was her right to find love. She did not want her husband to know about it and was not ready to talk about it in therapy. She never saw that relationship as a sin or as cheating, since she never had sex with her lover. Therapy terminated after a few sessions when it became clear that each of the couple's goal in therapy continued to be in a different direction: The husband insisted on trying to improve his marriage, while the wife insisted on getting a divorce. The husband recruited his wife's parents to continue forcing their daughter to accept her marriage. The wife surrendered but kept her affair as a "fair compensation." The wife's openness to legitimate her affair is very rare among Arab women. In general, when women feel that they cannot be free to feel their own personal emotions they become more frustrated with their own private families and with the social status of Arab women in general.

Arab society relates differentially to men's feeling in comparison with women's. Arab society, including professionals such as doctors, therapists, and lawyers, try to "fix" any deprivation from which a man may suffer. For instance, when the wife suffers from frigidity, which leads to abstinence from being involved in sexual relations with her husband, everyone—his family, her family, and doctors—intervene to "fix" the situation for the well-being of the husband. In the opposite case, when a man suffers from any sort of sexual dysfunction that leads them to abstain from sex, his family and the wife's family will try to silence the wife, make her feel guilty for complaining, and ask her to accept the situation as her destiny and repress her sexual needs.

When such women come to therapy, besides receiving empathy for their situation, they can discuss whether to seek a divorce or to find alternative paths to sexual satisfaction. Arab women prefer to remain in bad marriages rather than to divorce. The status of divorced women is very low; many of them will have no second chance of getting married, or a second marriage could worsen their social class status and their mental well-being, if they are forced to marry an older or abusive man. As for finding alternative ways to get sexual satisfaction, such as autosatisfaction, many Arab women lack basic sex education. They misjudge any unfamiliar sexual behavior as forbidden by their religion.

MARRIAGE AND FAITH

According to the Islamic faith, marriage is complementary to religious obligations. Men and women are encouraged to marry as a way of maintaining their chastity and as a remedy for sexual deviation (Abu-Baker, 2002). Although divorce is considered abominable, Islam allows it if one or both spouses find it impossible to accept the other as a partner. Nevertheless, the rate of divorce in the Arab world is about 4% (Barakat, 1993; Fargness, 1996). Arab couples try to repair marriages rather than divorce, since divorce may denigrate the reputation of both extended families (Simon, 1996).

Most marriages are arranged by family members or friends. Because marriage is construed as a relationship between two extended families, it has to be examined in depth before any serious steps are taken. "Arabs generally approach marriage with more pragmatism, based on group consensus rather than individual choice" (Abudabbeh & Nydell, 1993). From marriage, the couple seeks companionship and love, financial security, social status, and children. They often focus on the children's issues, whether they are still small or adults, rather than on their own romantic needs (Simon, 1996).

Nehaya's story illustrates the ideology of marriage as a remedy for sexual deviation and cultural practices. She is a housewife and widow who has four children. Her husband, who was also her cousin, died 7 years ago, when Nehaya was 24 years old. Her family of origin suggested that Nehaya marry her brother-in-law, a preferred practice in traditional Arab societies (Muslim and Christian). Nehaya refused, since the brother-in-law was much older than she and married with children, and she did not want to be his second wife. Nehaya begged to be allowed to live alone with her children. Two years after the death of the husband, when Nehaya was 26, she came to therapy. Among the problems she faced during that period were her emotional loneliness and the lack of sex in her life. When autosatisfaction was introduced to her, Nehaya was afraid that she was going to commit a sin. She was guided to read various Islamic attitudes regarding this subject; some related to it as sin, others related to it as preventing sin (it would preclude her being involved in out-of-wedlock sex). Nehaya adopted the attitude which allowed masturbation. This reduced some of the tension in her life.

Concerning other problems that arose after the death of her husband, Nehaya was encouraged to continue her high school education, to learn from her accountant how to deal with her money, and to consult with her therapist regarding the upbringing of her children. Men in her extended family tried constantly to take control of Nehaya's life and money; however, she learned acceptable traditional strategies to continue dealing independently with her life, while at the same time showing symbolic respect to elders in her extended family. The fact that Nehaya inherited money from her husband and did not need financial support gave her a kind of power: Because husbands or other males (brothers, older sons, fathers) are supposed to be the breadwinners and the disciplinary figures in Arab families (Budman, Lipson, & Meleis, 1992), she could ask the men who wanted to control her life to support her financially. However, they did not want to pay to support Nehaya; they just wanted to enforce their traditional control over her. Her traditional financial support neutralized their traditional authority.

According to Arabic traditions, women have to maintain a low profile and display submissiveness in public even though in some families women are the main breadwinners and decision makers in the privacy of their homes (Simon, 1996). Alldredge (1984) finds that a couple's level of education is usually reflected in their style of decision making: The more educated they both are, the more they share in the decision-making process. However, they still retain the notion that the male has the "last word." In less educated couples, women make the decisions concerning the necessities of daily life in their household and for their children, while males make other kinds of decisions. During the therapist's work with Nehaya, she invested in her education, in learning to control her life, her children, and her finances. In 2 years she became more educated and more successful in directing her family and life than her male siblings. The more successful she became, the less suitable they found it to control her. On the other hand, she left all types of negotiating with male handymen, who came to her home to take care of household repairs, to her brothers. Both the brothers and the handymen treasured Nehaya's respect of tradition, which did not allow her to be alone at home with strange men. They became convinced of the high quality of her value system. She also invited her brothers to her children's ceremonies at school. All parties were happy with this arrangement.

DIFFERENT ATTITUDES TOWARD MENTAL HEALTH FOR MEN AND WOMEN

A very small percentage of women who need therapy seek it immediately. Women are usually cautious about declaring their need to be in therapy to avoid being deemed "crazy" or "wasting the family's money." Some other families are embarrassed by the poor mental health of the women. Arab families relate to men's need to mental health services as a necessity. For instance, a sister three times took a loan, each time equivalent to her annual salary, to send her addicted brother to therapy, while an Arab family is potentially ready to kill, abandon, or punish in other ways a daughter who becomes addicted. In couple's therapy, the wife of an obsessive-jealous husband reduced her sphere of activities to home and work in an attempt to regain his confidence in her. She was a social worker herself and his attitude distracted her from concentrating on her work. The husband and both his extended family and hers advised her to keep a low profile and demonstrate acceptance of her husband's behavior. In another case, the wife suspected that her husband was having affairs with women with whom he would talk on his mobile phone. After a tremendous fight their relatives recommended that they should try therapy. He threatened in therapy that if she did not behave herself he would soon "send her back to her family of origin."

Women, as a result of the psychology of oppression, are not always sensitive to the psychological needs of other women. Some mothers are willing to bring their daughters to therapy secretly, but only when lack of therapy would bring social shame to the entire extended family, as in cases of rape. In such conditions, the secrecy, the responsibility the victim carries for the well-being of the extended family, and the lack of real family support together lead to a situation of "secondary victimization" for the victim. In such cases, therapy becomes the only source of support. Ignorance of the fundamentals of mental health, on the one hand, and the low status of Arab women, on the other, lead to such neglect of the mental needs of women.

A 30-year-old married female kleptomaniac was brought to therapy by her mother and sister. "I wish she were dead instead of being a thief," said the mother in front of her daughters to express her shame at the behavior of her daughter. The mother was under stress in case the in-laws of her daughter became aware of her situation. In the course of the session, the mother described her husband and her oldest son as being adulterers. When I asked about the religious sin and the social shame of their behavior, the mother said: "They are men. They will not be judged like she will be for her behavior. She may be thrown out of her home. I couldn't throw my husband out for adultery; nor would my daughter-in-law."

LACK OF INDEPENDENCE

The mental health of Arab women is related to the social judgment of the society in which they live. This is considered another major source of stress from which women clients suffer and which they take into consideration while attending therapy. Rarely are women considered mature and able to be independent at any age. For example, Dema, a graduate student who started school after saving the money that she earned for a few years, suffered from her relationship with her parents who wanted to control her behavior because she "has no husband who should have authority over her." Dema was furious about her parents who, on the one hand, behaved as modern parents and allowed their daughter to work late, but on the other hand, wanted to be traditional by controlling Dema's decisions and free time. Had they been traditional parents, they would have had to support Dema financially, besides providing help with all her other needs. Dema had a professional diploma in tourism, a profession in which she had worked for the last 9 years, and had recently graduated from the department of social studies at a university. At this stage in her life Dema was more educated than her parents and all her four siblings. Although she was 32, since she had never been married, her father and her two male brothers considered themselves custodians of her life. Dema struggled to widen the margins of her personal freedom. Her family considered her ability to go to work and school a wide enough range of personal freedom. They wanted her to ask their permission for any additional activity. Controlling Dema's free time was the focus of the family disputes that took place between her and her family members. Dema could not claim the need to be free since that would have been interpreted as "wanting to be arrogant and not modest." Although Arab families have mostly changed their attitudes toward women, they still use honor and modesty as controlling issues, especially when the type of change occurring in the life of women interferes with the male authority in traditional families. While Dema's family controlled her movement, it was very difficult for Dema to meet suitable men whom she could marry. During her early twenties, Dema had refused all suggestions of an arranged marriage; her relatives considered her rebellious and stopped trying to find her a good match. In her job she worked mainly with foreigners, whom she found more democratic and easy to live with. However, her family made it clear to her that she would never have their permission to marry a non-Arab or a man who belonged to another faith. Since Dema started her higher education at the age of 28, she did not meet Arab men her age in college. Most of the male students were in their late teens or early twenties. During these years Dema found that the best way to meet men was during the hours she was supposed to be at work or in school, without her parents' knowledge or permission. This left Dema with the feeling of being dishonest and lying. The dissonance in which she lived for a long time caused her psychological distress and family disputes. In therapy she blamed her family and her society and its norms for her condition.

In cases such as this, therapy should both empower the client and also be aware of the sociocultural characteristics of the politics of gender relations. Dema's dream was to leave her parents' house and live by herself. Nevertheless, she was not able to process this idea since she was aware that unmarried individuals in the Middle East should stay in the parents' residence until marriage, when a change in their social status and in their relation toward independence would emerge. As an unmarried woman, Dema also was not allowed to discuss her sexual needs with her family or friends. In fact, it is rare that Arab women talk openly about their sexual needs (Abu-Baker, 2002). According to religious rules and social norms, Arabs and Muslims are not allowed to have sexual relations out of wedlock. People, especially unmarried young men, maintain sexual relations secretly. However, they are not allowed to live with a girlfriend in their traditional villages. In rare cases, Arab or Muslim men will cohabitat with non-Arab women. Sexual needs are among the important reasons for early marriage in the Arab world (Abu-Baker, in press-a).

SEX THERAPY FOR ARAB/MUSLIM COUPLES

Traditionally, not religiously, sex is conceptualized as a man's need that the wife has to provide. The notion of intimacy often has a nonsexual nuance. Old couples relate to intimacy as companionship, keeping each other's secrets and demonstrating respect in public. Arab couples do not talk regularly about sex in order to maintain chaste behavior. Couples and families voice their experiences and opinions about sexual relations between couples only when a problem arises. Sexual problems from which women commonly suffer and for which they seek therapy are vaginismus and sexual desire disorder. Individual sessions with this group of women reveals one or more of the following circumstances: (a) an intimidating upbringing regarding sex—sex is viewed as a tool to maintain and internalize chaste behavior; (b) forced marriage with no love or intimacy developing between the couple; (c) silencing of the women's feelings toward abusive relations they have experienced with their husbands. In all cases, a change in the type of relationship between the couple has to occur in order to alleviate the sexual problems of this group of women.

It is unusual for an Arab man to talk about sex with a woman who is not his wife; therefore, having a conversation with a female therapist regarding this topic is a strange situation for him. Further, this talk may invite traditional talk and a traditional reaction to the clinical setting. In order to prepare the ground for a talk which will be beneficial, a correct therapist-client relationship should first be developed between the parties. When married women complain about abuse, citing the sexual claims of their husbands, a distorted view of religious Islamic verses is clear to see. The following case illustrates the intertwined relation between gender norms, social control, marital problems, and sexual frustration.

Taroob came to therapy as a result of a nervous breakdown and depression. She was 45-years-old and her husband, who was also her cousin, was 5 years older. They had been married for 27 years. Her husband initiated marital therapy because he was frustrated with her depression. In an individual session Taroob revealed a history of sexual, psychological, and verbal abuse. Ebraheem, the husband, who was a teacher in his village, had forced his decisions on his wife. Little by little he had forced her to stay in the house, not leaving it without his permission and without his accompanying her. Ebraheem was a jealous man who lacked self-confidence. From the early stages of their marriage, when Taroob wanted to go out, or when she refused to have sex, Ebraheem interpreted her behavior as having an affair. Gradually Taroob chose to follow Ebraheem's demands obediently in order to prevent his suspicions and blame. Two months before her nervous breakdown, their daughter got engaged to a young man from another village (continuing, however, to live with her parents and abstain from sexual relations as traditions require). Ebraheem suspected a "secret relationship" between his daughter and her fiancé (meaning having a sexual relationship). After the engagement he started to put pressure on his wife, asking her to convince their daughter to leave her fiancé. Taroob realized that Ebraheem would extend his suspicions and jealousy to include the intimate life of their daughter. Taroob left their bedroom and stayed in her children's room for 2 months. During this period she continued to serve all Ebraheem's needs, except sex. In therapy she cried and asked whether she had to force herself to have sex with him. It was revealed that for the last 8 years Taroob had related to Ebraheem's sexual demands as daily rape, which she had to force herself to accept in order to be able to live in her home peacefully.

It is unacceptable for Arabs and not in accordance with Islam to use the term *rape* when describing sexual relations between a husband and his wife. However, the sayings of the prophet Mohammed taught men not to have forced sexual relations with their wives. In the case of Ebraheem, many religious and traditional sayings were quoted in order to show him his behavior was unacceptable. "Should I surrender to his demands?" asked Taroob in therapy with tears; "Should I give him my body while I hate him, hate his behavior, hate his authority, but am not able to show any of these feelings because I do not have a profession and do not have anywhere to go?" She was encouraged to express her feelings and thoughts. Arab women who move from the status of mothers to the status of mothers-in-law and grandmothers gain additional social respect. Taroob was encouraged to regain ownership of her body and sexuality. She was encouraged to read prophet Mohammed's sayings and stories regarding healthy marital relations. Taroob wanted to feel safe from Ebraheem's abuse.

Therapy with couples like Ebraheem and Taroob should focus on seeing each one of them alone for individual therapy before moving to couple's therapy. In addition to psychological problems from which Ebraheem suffered, he had to train himself to be empathic to the needs of his wife, including her need to be silent. Most Arab men have been brought up believing that women exist for them. Some Arab women describe good men as "not being bad, not being physically or psychologically abusive." This description reflects the low expectations of sympathy and support women have from their husbands. Husbands such as Ebraheem hear in therapy a new terminology when discussing their abilities to respect and support women's emotions and free will. At the same time, wives such as Taroob should be empowered and encouraged to reclaim responsibilities for their lives, bodies, and families.

THE MENTAL HEALTH OF IMMIGRANT WOMEN

Compared with the amount of anthropological and sociological research on Arabs in the Middle East, very few studies have been written about the mental health of Arab immigrants in America (Abudabbeh, 1996; Meleis, 1981). After the Gulf War, and as a result of the traumatized Arab immigrant population, a few more research reports were published (Abu-Baker, 1997; Abudabbeh & Nydell, 1993; Jamil et al., 2002; Nobles & Sciarra, 2000; Moradi & Hasan, 2004). Findings of this research emphasize the social isolation Arab immigrants feel in the United States and the fear of rejection which individuals experience in workplaces, schools, and social settings. As a result, families constantly discuss ways to compensate for their members' sense of lacking acceptance and belonging, which is in itself an act that aggravates their anxiety. The main solution most immigrants find useful is emphasizing their belonging to their homelands.

Emigration in itself is a traumatic event that influences individuals for the rest of their lives (Grinberg & Grinberg, 1984/1989). Often, immigration to the United States becomes an obsessive idea, and is perceived as an ideal solution for a problematic situation. Often men leave their wives and children in their homeland, emigrate alone, and struggle with financial conditions and official paperwork until reaching the day, typically between 2 to 8 years later, when they are able to reunite with their wives and children in the United States. Some other immigrants never succeed in bringing their families to the United States, forcing them to live apart for the rest of their lives.

Fareed's wife (see Chapter 3 for Fareed's story) was forced to stay in Jordan for about 4 years. Fareed sent his father $200 each month for his wife, Umaya, who had to wait patiently for her husband to succeed. Meanwhile, Umaya became a semisingle mother, who had to take care of her four children by herself. And as a semi-independent wife, her father-in-law refused to give her the whole amount of her monthly allowance, but rather obliged her to ask him for each and every item she wanted to buy for herself or her children. The emigration of her husband decreased the social status of Umaya, who suddenly became "without husband," and the father-in-law enforced his authority over her. In the meantime, the husband had to prove that he had steady work and income, and a clean criminal record. Fareed had to hire a lawyer to help him understand the intensive legal requirements he had to fulfill. In return, he had to pay the lawyer a high portion of his poor savings, which constantly delayed the date when he could send for his family.

For 4 years Umaya struggled and urged her husband to finish his paperwork and let her and her children follow him. When they succeeded, Umaya found out that her husband had bought a very small apartment in a multicultural poor neighborhood. She had no driving license. He pushed her to pass the driving exam in order to drive their children to their schools. He asked some of his friends to teach her the driving laws in English. She was under great stress. A week before the opening of the school year, the wife of a friend directed her back and forth from her home to her children's schools. Umaya was frightened by the street systems and consequently developed agoraphobia. For years she was unable to drive outside the small area she was familiar with, within which she could drive to her children's schools, the supermarket, and a few friends.

Isolation and Language Difficulties

Over the years, Umaya experienced constant struggles to function as a responsible mother vis-à-vis the school system. Alas, she never succeeded in fully understanding conversations with the teachers. Umaya struggled to take back full responsibility for her children's life. In order to understand the teachers, she asked an Arab friend who was brought up in the United States to accompany her and translate the conversation for her. The friend did. However, this experience left Umaya with a sense of worthless and helplessness. She believed then that it would take her a long time to gain complete command of the English language and, accordingly, of her family and life in the United States. The subjects discussed in conferences with the teachers were linked directly to the difficulties of immigration her children faced, such as mastering the language, integrating with their classmates, and participating in social activities. Umaya was not able to help in any of these areas. Each additional encounter with the larger systems such as hospitals, the immigration office, and so forth, depleted more of Umaya's self-confidence, since she found the terminology and the system in itself very unfamiliar. She felt that she had become a burden on her friend who accompanied her to all these necessary meetings. On the other hand, Umaya was forced to share all private matters of her family with this friend without any ability to protect her privacy.

Even living in the United States with her husband, Umaya continued to feel like a semisingle mother. Her husband, who wanted to fulfill the "American dream"—which to him meant moving from entrenched poverty in the Middle East to an American middle-class lifestyle—had forced himself to work a full-time job as a garage mechanic from 6 a.m. to 5 p.m., and then do private garage work in the evening. She had to take care of the needs of the children and of the house by herself. She was very lonely. Phone calls to Jordan were very expensive and her husband blamed her for them. The only refuge she found was the morning coffee meetings she had with a few Arab women immigrants from the Middle East and twice-a-week shopping in the Middle Eastern grocery where she could always find other Arabs, talk to them, and extend her social circle. There were also Saturday visits to the Islamic Center where children of Arab immigrants learned writing and reading Arabic, attended courses in Islam religion, and socialized with other Arab and Muslim children, while she could socialize with women living in conditions similar to her own. Husbands accompanied them to the Islamic center only on Islamic religious holidays.

Despite all the improvement in her English over the years, Umaya eventually found that she could not even have a meaningful conversation with her 12-

year-old daughter. When Umaya wanted to speak with her daughter about puberty and adolescence, she did not have the vocabulary in English. And after 6 years in America her older daughter, and all the other children, could understand only Arabic "home-need" language; that is they knew how to have a conversation regarding food or other daily issues related to their family. Again Umaya felt lonely within her own household and family. The children related to the school system as the main source of education, while they related to their family as the main source of restrictions. The parents expected their children to obey them fully, while the children were raised in the school system to ask questions, to discuss, to expect to understand what had been said to them.

In the Middle East the phenomenon of teenagers is a new one. Until 50 years ago, the age for marriage in most Arab societies was 14–16 for girls and 16–18 for boys. Many children—male and female—had to work in the family fields or household after school, leaving no free time for them to develop their own subculture. Changes that have taken place in the Middle East, especially obligatory education for all children and the postponement of the age of marriage for both genders (17 for females and 18 for males), now keeps more children together in the school system. Moreover, free access to media from all over the world, especially the English-speaking West, has helped the subculture of teenagers penetrate Arab societies. Therefore, the teenage lifestyle is a new experience for Arab parents, who with the help of teachers in the school system try to control their teenagers. Nevertheless, this experience is more intense for Arab parents who live in America, since Western parents allow their children more freedom and independence in comparison with their Arab counterparts in the Middle East.

Children in Transition

A major problem for immigrant families is that children are acculturated faster than their parents in American society, a tendency that causes children and their parents to have conflicting points of view (Barazangi, 1996). Investigating the perception and practice of Islam in North America, Barazangi (1996) concluded that "Arab youth are being reared in two different environments at the same time, the familial and communal Muslim or nationalistic Arab and the school or host-societal secular" (p. 133).

Umaya's children and those of other Arab American immigrants belong simultaneously to two dissonant cultures, which causes social and psychological stress for these children who have been born or brought up for most of their lives in the West. Eisenlohr (1996) described their condition as being expected to behave as Westerners during the day and as Arabs at night. The transition is not always easy, especially when daily life praxis carries a fundamental contradiction between the two cultures. Parents, especially mothers, complain that they should be able to trace their children's behavior and correct it whenever any Westernized behavior is evident, such as drinking alcohol, having relationships with the opposite sex, rebellion against parents, and so forth. Sometimes the struggle between parents and their teenage children is manifested in daily quarrels. When this happens, the social control of the close-knit community helps parents with this mission, especially when gathering with all Arab teenagers in the Islamic Center.

Umaya, her husband, and other Arab parents in their social circle judge American society to have a negative influence on their children. For the last 3 years, Umaya has saved every available penny and leaves with her children on the first day of their summer vacation to go to her hometown where they stay about 3 months. Umaya and other parents believe that this is the best means to keep Arab children away from "negative American influences" and, in effect, give the children an intensive workshop in Arabic language, the Islamic religion, and traditional norms. It also lets cousins get to know each other for future in-group marriages. This plan keeps Umaya happy; she has an intensive social and family life for 3 months. Her husband visits for the last 10 days, and then they all travel back together. The financial price Umaya's family pays for this annual visit (tickets and gifts) prevents the family from having any other savings.

During Umaya's last visit to her hometown, her daughter, who was 13 years old, decided to wear the Islamic veil, as she had seen most of her peers doing. Umaya, her husband, and the extended family were very pleased with this decision. The daughter explained her decision as freeing herself from the obligation of explaining to her friends in America why she was not able to share in their after-school activities; she believed they would leave her alone when they saw her *hijab* veil. Umaya then felt obliged to veil herself, since otherwise her social circle would criticize her. Umaya summarized that, paradoxically, immigration to the West caused her and her family to be more religious and more traditional.

Different Expectations About Teenage Daughters

The primary concern of most Arab parents in the United States is for their daughters' reputation. The Arab community expects all teenagers to follow the cultural norms strictly, otherwise they will be punished by the propagation of rumors which will ruin their future chances to marry or be accepted by the community. Parents, brothers, married sisters, and uncles keep their eyes on the daughters in the family. Usually, traditional Arab families do not allow high school female students to participate in after-school activities where boys are involved or if transportation is not promised by the school system. Any sport activity that compels girls to show their bodies, such as swimming and tennis, is also not allowed by these families. When girls in such families are caught having relationships with boyfriends, typically they are beaten and prohibited from attending school. In cases of lost reputation in the Arab community—for instance, for doing drugs or having out-of-wedlock sex—girls are sent back to their homeland to find husbands. Those parents who allow their daughters to participate in activities, have American friends, or work after school, implore their daughters to behave according to the norm of the Arabic culture in order not to evoke community criticism against the family. Community criticism may classify the daughter as an "outcast" (Eisenlohr, 1996, p. 262). Eisenlohr claims that as a result of the severe restrictions, some teenage girls lie to their parents, attend school without wearing the cultural/religious scarf, and skip some classes to meet boys and girls. A dissonance exists between parents and daughters, and between parents and school, in terms of each other's expectations.

There are both commonalities and dissimilarities throughout the Middle Eastern Arab countries regarding the practice of Arab heritage and culture, as is also the case regarding understanding, interpreting, and practicing Islam. Thus Arabs carry these similarities and differences with them to their countries of immigration. When a heterogeneous Arab community decides to treat their children according to the Islamic or Arab heritage and culture, they have to decide according to which aspects of each and how. This is one of the main problems facing parents who want to carry on their traditions in the host country.

When Umaya meets other women in the Islamic Center an ongoing debate develops between women from various Arab countries and with various educational backgrounds, ages and social status regarding the best ways to bring up children, both boys and girls, in the United States. The absence of the extended family in the United States makes it more important for Arab families to consult each other about their daily life problems when they meet in their social gatherings with family and friends. As a result, immigration has added a new role to imams (religious leaders), unknown in the Arab countries, as family counselors. Lacking the necessary training, these imams provide Islamic answers based on theological law, which do not serve the needs of second- and third-generation Arab Muslims (Haddad, 1983). This type of discussion does not help Umaya to make decisions regarding the best path for her children. The debates make her even more confused than she is when she compares the Arabic and the American ways. After consulting with the Imam regarding family therapy, Umaya went to therapy to seek "final words" (her expression) for the education of her children in this foreign country and culture.

Therapy helped Umaya to regain confidence. When asked to compare her knowledge of the English language while in her homeland and now, she recognized the large steps she had made over the years. She was encouraged to relate to herself as an expert in her children's life, as a mediator between Arabic culture and her children, while at the same time she began relating to her children as mediators of American culture. Also she gained more confidence in herself as an Arabic teacher at the Islamic Center. Umaya's confidence encouraged her to start driving longer distances. Also, she was encouraged to explore more of her new American cultural context and to test her new experiences with an open mind, without stereotyping. By the end of therapy, she was no longer in fear of her town, of the American culture, or of the dissimilarities in her children's behavior in comparison to their counterparts in Arab countries. At the same time, she was encouraged to utilize the genuine support system of her natural social net (Arab community and Islamic Center). Umaya was content with the results of therapy. She talked about its importance at the Islamic Center to the imam and other women. She related to it as "consultation with an expert." Four other families from the same center reached therapy as a result of Umaya's encouragement.

Umaya's goal is to return home when her younger son finishes high school. Then the family can live respectably on the husband's pension. However, Umaya's children believe that they like to visit Jordan, but they are too Americanized to accept the university or the work system there. They insist on continuing to live in the United States. Probably Umaya will be able to force her two daughters to immigrate back home with her, but not her sons. Grinberg and Grinberg (1984/1989) stated that once a person becomes an immigrant, he sentences himself to remain in an immigrant psychological state for the rest of his life. Whether they continue living in the host country or they decide to go back to their home country, they become in both places "extraterrestrial," psychologically and socially speaking.

SUMMARY

Working with Arab clients from many Arab countries, I adopted the philosophical essence of the anthrotherapist stance, similar to what Chenail and Morris (1995) called "the researching therapist" stance. Gathering ethnographic data helps one to learn about the social reality of the clients, including their cultural background, ecology, and relationship with the larger systems. This helps to relate empathically to clients' distress and to comprehend it according to its suitable context. Later, this ethnographic information enables therapists to ask clients questions about some themes that have special importance in their social settings. Furthermore, it helps assess culturally bonded behavior as "normal and acceptable" in the clients' natural setting. It prevents therapists from pathologizing their immigrant clients' reality.

In order to be able to help clients deal with the confusion in their lives created by the cultural contradictions among their multiple contexts, I had to learn about each one of these contexts. This knowledge helps the therapist empathize with their experiences. Furthermore, therapists' awareness of the usage of cultural self in therapy helps them utilize the understanding of the ethnic component of the family. When therapists acknowledge the relativity of their own cultural values, it helps them respect more cultural differences. It is highly recommended that therapists adopt what I call the anthrotherapist approach.

NOTE

1. Parts of this chapter are based on a Ph.D. thesis written in the School of Social and Systemic Studies, Nova Southeastern University, Fort Lauderdale, FL (see Abu-Baker, 1997).

Chapter 11

Indirect Therapy: Metaphor Therapy

It was emphasized in Chapters 8 and 9 that making what is unconscious conscious and helping the client fulfill his or her authentic self or to be more assertive may open up, or in some cases initiate, an irresolvable intrafamilial conflict. Therefore, therapists would do better, when working with Arab/Muslim immigrants, to consider indirect intervention that would avoid interpretations and insights or extreme changes in the client's interpersonal behavior. In addition, given the special appreciation that Arab/Muslim people give to visions and metaphors, metaphor therapy, bibliotherapy, and symbolic rituals may be a therapy of choice for many clients.

IMAGINATION AND METAPHORS
IN THE ARAB/MUSLIM CULTURE

In his article titled "The Illusion of Reality or the Reality of Illusion: Hallucination and Culture," Al-Issa (1995) explains the differences in the attitude toward reality between the West and the East. Many Eastern societies, including Arabs/Muslims, consider imagination a part of their normal daily life. Instead of pathologizing hallucinations and delusions, as Westerners do, they consider them to be guidance to the "real reality." Crucial decisions in peoples' lives are influenced by the meanings given to visions and dreams, and people who are familiar with these experiences and meanings are considered wise, and their advice is often sought by others. For many people in these societies the objective reality is the false reality, and therefore they pray and meditate in order to come closer to that "real reality" (Dwairy, 1997a).

Arabic language is very metaphoric and the Qur'anic verses include many metaphoric directives (Hourani, 1983, 1991). *Qeyas* (or knowing through mensuration or measurement), which is mentioned in Chapter 2 as one major mechanism in the Arab/Muslim mind, is in fact the utilization of an indirect and metaphoric way of thinking. Instead of thinking directly about the concrete problem in its present context, the Muslim is directed to measure the present new problem or situation by a former similar one (stands as a metaphor) that had been addressed or answered by the Qur'an or Sunna. Based on this measurement, the Muslim applies the old answer or solution to the new problem and behaves accordingly.

Given the central role of imagination and metaphors in their lives, Arab/ Muslim clients are expected to describe their experience in imaginative and metaphoric language. Instead of saying "others cannot understand my own suffering" an Arab/Muslim client may mention a proverb such as *"Elli eidu belmay mesh methl elli eidu bennar"* [the one whose hand is in water is not like the one whose hand is in fire]. When describing her feeling of losing control, an Arab/Muslim woman may say: "My world is collapsing over my head," or when she describes her distress she may say: "My heart is burning and my head is exploding." When therapists encounter these expressions, should they ask the client to translate these expressions into more objective or psychological terms? May they utilize these expressions in a metaphoric therapy?

A BIOPSYCHOSOCIAL MODEL OF METAPHOR THERAPY

Metaphors are used and understood in a variety of ways in psychotherapy. According to psychoanalysis, metaphors and images are considered symbols that need to be interpreted and understood in order to gain insights and self-awareness. Alternatively, one may consider metaphorical language to be another legitimate mode of communication, which influences the mind and the body. As such, metaphor may be utilized in therapy to achieve change in the clients' experiences, without directly bringing unconscious forbidden contents to the consciousness.

In my biopsychosocial model of metaphor therapy (Dwairy, 1997a), I describe three pathways that connect the positivistic biological, psychological, and social levels of experience with the metaphoric and imaginative level. According to this model, psychological experiences such as anxiety, anger, or happiness are translated through an unconscious process of symbolization into images or metaphors. This process of symbolization is influenced by the personal as well as by the collective experience, so that many culturally specific proverbs, idioms, or myths become incorporated in the personal images and metaphors. For instance, depression is associated for Arabs with the color black, while for Americans it may be associated with blue. In addition to these two pathways (psychological and cultural communications) between the positivistic experience and the metaphor level, a third, biological, pathway that involves neurotransmitters, hormones, and peptides connects the two levels of experience (see Figure 11.1). This model assumes two-way communication between the biopsychosocial and the metaphor level of experience. Accordingly, depressive experience

Figure 11.1. A Biopsychosocial Model of Metaphor Therapy

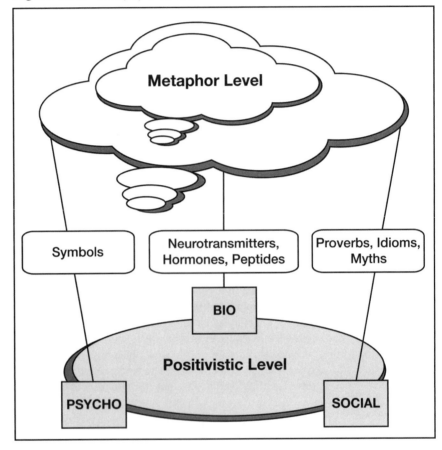

generates depressive images and metaphors, and vice versa. Changing the depressive images and metaphors necessarily changes the biopsychosocial experience of depression through the three pathways of communication. In other words, therapy that generates a change in images and metaphors does not stop there, and is not detached from the biopsychosocial real experience, but rather generates real and deep change in that experience through the three pathways of communication. Much of this two-way communication, which takes place through the personal and cultural symbolization process and through the biological communication, is unconscious, and it may therefore be useful for making real changes without revealing unconscious forbidden contents.

This model may explain a variety of therapeutic techniques that utilize imagination and metaphors. Kopp (1995) in his three-stage metaphor therapy first asks the client to describe the metaphor that describes the problem in concrete terms; in the second stage he asks her to change the metaphor in such a way that it describes the solution of the problem; and at the end the client is asked what she has learned from the metaphoric solution and what the practical implications are that could be utilized to cope with the problems. In fact, Kopp moves together with the client to the metaphor level to discuss and process the problem and the solution metaphorically. In the third stage he leads the client back to the personal biopsychosocial level to utilize what was learned from the metaphoric processing about the problem and the solution. Bresler (1984) directs his patients who suffer from chronic pain to control their pain by controlling the images in their minds. First, he guides his client to draw the pain on a piece of paper, then to draw the state of no pain, and then to draw the pleasure state. Through these three drawings the client processes the pain experience metaphorically. In the second stage Bresler teaches the client to control the images in her mind and to retain the pictures (images) of no pain and pleasure. This control in the metaphor level helps the client control the physical pain in the biopsychosocial level. The proposed model explains other therapeutic techniques such as guided imagery therapy, art therapy, and bibliotherapy (Dwairy 1997a). In all these therapies the client processes the problem and finds solutions or new coping strategies in the metaphoric level, which influence the biopsychosocial experience through the three pathways that connect the two levels of experience.

Based on the proposed model, the conscious discussion that brings the client from the metaphor level to the biopsychosocial level, as in Kopp's therapy, is optional and is not recommended when the therapist wants to avoid revealing unconscious and forbidden contents. Witztum and Goodman (2003) worked within the Jewish Ultra-Orthodox community. The distress of many of their clients was constructed as a dramatic narrative, inspired by shared cultural symbols, in which the clients were trapped in relationships with nonhuman figures. Instead of revealing the unconscious meanings of the clients' delusions and hallucinations, Witztum and Goodman helped them find and activate alternative plots that adhered to common cultural themes in their society, in which they became active agents. Their interventions were in the narrative imaginary level and included enacting some religious rituals. It was reported that these interventions worked without discussing the symbolic meanings of the narrative, images, or rituals and without psychodynamic interpretations. According to the proposed model, it seems that the narrative and ritualistic interventions sufficed to influence the positivistic biopsychosocial level of experience through the three connective pathways.

Imad: Metaphoric Coping Leads to Actual Change

Imad was 28-years-old. An older son of a Palestinian Arab/Muslim family, he suffered from severe depressive-somatic symptoms that started after his marriage 3 years before his arrival in therapy. When he declared his intention to marry the girl who later became his wife, his family rejected the proposed bride and disapproved of the marriage. In an unusual step, the marriage took place against the will of the family, which therefore ostracized the couple. This ostracism was unbearable while Imad continued to work in the family restaurant and live with his wife in the family house, one floor above his parents, and share the same quarters as the whole extended family.

For 3 years Imad was caught in feelings of severe guilt, shame, and loneliness. He was not able to enjoy his marriage, and his relationship with his wife became tense. In therapy he consistently justified the attitude of his family and was unable to express any dissatisfaction or anger toward them. In the previous year, his second brother had married. The family celebrated the marriage in the family house for a week, but Imad was not invited and would have been unable to attend anyway because he was hospitalized with a severe asthma attack.

When Imad came closer to expressing anger toward his family in therapy, he became rather anxious and tense, and changed the subject. In other words he was not capable of becoming conscious of unacceptable repressed feelings against the family. In one of the sessions he described his experience metaphorically, saying, "I feel as if I am circling around myself." This expression is common among Arabs when they want to express a state of being trapped, and was his metaphorical way of expressing his biopsychosocial experience. I moved with him into that metaphor and asked him to describe himself while he is "circling around" himself.

Imad: I am closed inside a round high wall and running around with no way out. I feel suffocated and tired.
Therapist: What other things do you see inside?
Imad: Nothing, I am alone there.
Therapist: Will you look to both sides and behind you and tell me what is there.
Imad: I see some rocks and a dry tree behind me.
Therapist: What do you see above you?
Imad: Blue sky and few white clouds.

At this moment the client let out a sigh of relief, indicating that widening the zoom of the metaphor had influenced the biology and psychology of his state.

Therapist: What do you want to do in this place?
Imad: I want to get out of here.
Therapist: Can you climb the walls?
Imad: No, they are too high.

Therapist: Can you use the rocks or the dry tree to help you climb them?
Imad: No, the branches are too short and thin.

Imad continued contemplating and wondering about this image for a couple of minutes.

Therapist: Your situation reminds me of some Palestinian prisoners who struggled to escape from an Israeli prison.
Imad: Yes, I may rot here, like them.
Therapist: Yes, but some of them found their way out.

The therapist was hinting at the well-known method of escaping from prison by digging a tunnel.

Imad: You mean those who dug tunnels?
Therapist: Yes.
Imad: How can I do that?
Therapist: Right, you need to think how can you do that?

Imad thought for a couple of minutes before speaking.

Imad: I might use these branches to dig. It is not easy but I can try.
Therapist: Yes, go ahead and do it.
Imad: It is not easy, but I will do it.
Therapist: It may take some time; but because you really want to get out, you can do it.

For several minutes Imad processed the image of digging.

Imad: I see the other side. I am almost out.
Therapist: What do you see?

Imad described an open place with vegetation, hills, and houses. While he was describing the place, his face expressed deep relief, as did his tone of voice. He continued to wander around and explore the place and to enjoy it for several minutes until the end of the session.

Before he left, we talked about his feeling of relief, but without addressing the symbolic meaning of the walls, rocks, or tree and the meaning of being outside the walls. We did not talk about ways of implementing the metaphoric solution in his real life. Based on the proposed model, one can assume that the metaphoric processing had made its effect unconsciously through the three connecting pathways. In the next session, he reported that he felt better and said that for several days he had been thinking of moving with his wife to Tel Aviv

(80 kilometers away from the village) to work in a restaurant there. Interestingly, he explained this plan as the best both for him and for his family. Within 2 weeks he moved with his wife to Tel Aviv. In a follow-up meeting after 3 months, both of them reported relief from the depressive-somatic symptoms. Their relationship became better and they considered having a baby.

This case indicates that a real change in the biopsychosocial life of the client can take place without revealing the unconscious-forbidden feelings toward the family, or without making "big" changes toward self-actualization. Imad got relief while he continued to believe that he was a good son of a good caring family. This belief seemed to be more crucial for his health than gaining insight about his repressed feelings of anger.

Would it have been possible to reach this solution of moving away from his family through direct discussion concerning his authentic feelings and attitudes toward his family? Probably, but such a direct way might have encountered a lot of resistance, and resulted in an intensification of symptoms or the client's dropping out of therapy.

SYMBOLIC RITUALS WITH SIGNIFICANT OBJECTS

In Chapter 6 I described the assessment technique called TASO, in which the client is directed to bring a significant object or item from his physical environment in order to talk about it in therapy. Talking about a significant object typically brings out significant memories and emotions that are related to a core conflict (Dwairy, 2001, 2003). According to the biopsychosocial model of metaphor therapy, one can consider the objects as metaphors or symbolic representation of a biopsychosocial experience, and therefore the discussion around the object is, in fact, a metaphoric processing of a significant problem or conflict. Accordingly, any change in the object-client relationship is associated with change in the biopsychosocial level of experience. Therefore, in addition to its diagnostic use, TASO can be employed to accomplish a therapeutic change without revealing forbidden unconscious contents (Dwairy, 2003).

After discussing the meaning of the object in terms of distress and conflicts, the therapist may move to a therapeutic stage by suggesting change in the object or in the object-client relationship. The therapist may ask: "Could you think about any change in this object, whether in its shape, location, or use? Could you think about putting it in a new place? Could you think about giving it to somebody?"

Samira: Using TASO as a Therapeutic Technique

Samira was a 27-year-old unmarried woman who suffered from low back pain. Her physician thought that she was "carrying a lot of stress on her back," and therefore referred her to psychotherapy. Samira was the second daughter of a large family with four daughters and three sons. She described a mutually disappointing relationship with her parents, who had passed away. Her father died 3 years before the referral to psychotherapy and her mother followed him after 2 years of coping with cancer. Since their deaths Samira had been experiencing a depressive condition: sadness, tiredness, hopelessness, and helplessness, which she associated with the increase of responsibility for her smaller brothers and sisters and to the worsening of her back pain since her parents' death.

When she was asked to bring a significant object to talk about in therapy she brought a tablecloth. Through this cloth she revealed a significant conflict with her parents around her need for a space of her own in the house. During elementary school she fought for a private study table and for a private closet in which to keep her personal items. Her parents, however, insisted on a shared collective style of living. The parents and the family members considered her an egoist who "cares only for herself." With much pain she described the family's discriminative and rejecting attitude toward her. In secondary school her relationship with her parents became more tense. She spent most of her time alone and preoccupied herself with handcrafts. She finished school with high grades and wanted to go to college. She said: "I wanted to live alone, away from them, more than I wanted to study." She worked for a year and saved some money. After a long struggle with her family, they agreed to let her study in a college 120 kilometers away from home. She rented a room and furnished it by herself. She asked her parents to bring a table from their house to her room. Only under pressure and after the intervention of her uncle did they agree. She said: "At last, after a long struggle, at age 20 I had my own bed, table, and closet."

While she talked about the tablecloth, she expressed, with many tears, her sorrow and anger toward her parents, who had not been supportive. On the other hand, she expressed guilt feelings because she was unable to experience or express any sympathy toward her parents who had passed away. She said, "I can't believe I am doing this to them. I wonder if I am causing pain to them where they are." As for her feelings about the tablecloth, she said that every time she saw it on the table, which was still in use, she got bad feelings, a mixture of sorrow and anger.

Instead of facilitating the expression of anger to her parents, which obviously would intensify her conflict and distress, the therapist tried to facilitate a symbolic action with the tablecloth. In other words, instead of finding a new order in the biopsychosocial level, the therapist facilitated a new order in the metaphoric level. The therapist asked: "Will you think whether there is anything you could do with this cloth other than putting it back on that table?" At this stage of the session she considered various options, such as storing it inside a closet, throwing it into the garbage, burning it, or giving it to her older married sister. She was not satisfied with any of these alternatives because they seemed to her too offensive. The therapist thought that an action was needed which would make a good balance between her anger and her guilt. He proposed that she take the tablecloth with two flowers to the graves of her parents and put the cloth on their grave and the two flowers on the cloth. On her way back she should go to a shop and buy a new tablecloth for the table. The idea seemed acceptable to Samira. At the next session she reported that she had done exactly what the therapist suggested, and said, "While I was doing this, I was unable to find anything to say to them; my mind was empty; I just cried until I found my way out of the cemetery." After this session Samira moved to a new stage in therapy, where she considered making new order in her life. Her depression and back pain started to calm down.

The therapist thought that this action expressed the two sides of her conflict: The act of returning the tablecloth to her parents was an expression of anger, and the act of putting two flowers on their grave alleviated her guilt feelings. According to the proposed model of metaphor therapy, one can assume that this symbolic action extended the metaphoric level of processing and was reflected unconsciously in the biopsychosocial level of her experience. This may explain the alleviation of her symptoms, despite the fact that therapy did not draw the negative feelings toward her parents out to her consciousness.

SUMMARY

When the level of individuation, ego strength, and family strictness indicate that the client cannot endure the intrafamilial conflicts that may be raised after revealing unconscious drives or feelings, therapists may consider indirect interventions that influence unconsciously the biopsychosocial level of experience. According to this model, the client's experience may be processed in two levels: the biopsychosocial level and the metaphoric level. The two levels are connected through three two-way pathways. Processing the problem in the metaphoric level in metaphor therapy, bibliotherapy, art therapy, rituals, or TASO influences the biopsychosocial level through the three two-way pathways that connect the two levels of experience. This model explains how the influence may take place without revealing the unconscious contents of the clients mind or without reaching insights through psychodynamic interpretations.

Conclusion

Practitioners who work with clients of Arab/Muslim descent in the West should expect to encounter some emotional, cognitive, and behavioral styles that are not typical to Western clients. Judging these styles according to Western theories may lead to a lot of misunderstandings on the part of the practitioners, and of alienation on the part of the clients. Of course, not all Arabs/Muslims are alike, but rather they are spread along a continuum from traditionalism to Westernization. In fact, the personality of most Arab/Muslim clients has a traditional portion and Western portion. The differing proportion of the two portions makes the cultural differences between the clients. The more traditional a client, the more his identity is collective.

This book is meant to help practitioners understand the traditional portion in the Arab/Muslim clients. The collective cultural background makes its impact in almost all areas of psychology. The psychosocial development of Arabs/Muslims who are more collective does not end in an independent autonomous personality; the distinctions within the intrapsychic components such as emotions, thoughts, and values and the distinction between the individual and her family is vague or absent. Collective Arab/Muslim clients are directed by an external control; they are concerned with social approval or sanctions; their interpersonal conflicts are more important than the intrapsychic ones; and they need social coping mechanisms more than defense mechanisms to solve the conflicts. These cultural features influence the clinical picture of many psychological disorders among traditional Arab/Muslim immigrants. Their distress is manifested in bodily complaints. Some of their normative behavior, such as psychological dependency or cultural delusions, may be pathologized by practitioners who are ignorant of the Arab/Muslim culture.

These cultural differences necessitate special attention when the Arab/Muslim client is evaluated, in order to gain a better understanding and to suit the therapy to her. Within this context, therapists should not be misled by formal factors such as gender, age, education, religiousness, or social role. Instead, level of individuation, ego strength, and strictness of the family are the important factors that need to be evaluated. Based on these three factors, clinicians and counselors can tailor the therapy to fit the client. In the case of a traditional client who is more dependent, has poor personal resources, and lives within a strict family, therapists are advised to avoid "digging" into the unconscious or intimate personal issues and avoid working to achieve independence, self-actualization, or assertiveness. Instead, it is recommended that they work with the family within a cultural empathy and regard, to help the client achieve better satisfaction and adaptation to the familial system. Therapists are advised to utilize members within the family and factors within the client's cultural system to enhance change. For these clients, indirect therapy such as metaphor therapy is recommended.

Once practitioners have acquired an understanding of the psychocultural characteristics of Arab/Muslims as a group, however, they should bear in mind the diversity among Arab/Muslim countries, genders, and ages, and the differences between urban and rural, and educated and uneducated people. Shared characteristics should not blind practitioners to the cross-cultural or individual differences that need to be sought in every client.

These reminders are important because when groups are discussed, it is difficult not to subtly adopt a stereotypic approach. This may be one of the inevitable costs of discussing group characteristics or even of conceptualizing several observations within one concept. It is necessary to draw attention to the error of generalization so that it will be perceived and avoided; I hope I have avoided such a generalization. One needs to keep individual differences in mind when learning about any group, such as gifted or depressive people. In every case, including that of Arabs/Muslims, one learns about what characterizes the group and what differentiates it from other groups. In addition to these between-group differences, one needs to keep seeing the within-group and individual differences.

The shared/collective characteristics of Arabs/Muslims described in this book are best considered as a cognitive framework or background against which counselors and therapists can interpret the results of their examination or understanding of a specific client. As always, the burden is on practitioners to identify the individual characteristics of their clients and locate them on a collective/shared cultural map—a process similar to when a clinical psychologist conducts a psychological assessment and relates the individual to the diagnostic map suggested by the DSM-IV. These maps are not the reality of clients, but rather are backgrounds to which practitioners may relate the reality of the client.

Based on the shared cultural characteristics of Arabs/Muslims and the cross-cultural differences presented in this book, I recommend that counselors and therapists revise the theories learned in developmental psychology, personality, assessment, psychodiagnosis, psychopathology, and psychotherapy. This culturally sensitive revision, as well as many of the ideas and applications presented in this book, may be applicable to many other non-Western groups such as Asians, Latin Americans, or Africans. Revising widely held notions about individuation, independence of the self or personality, centrality of the intrapsychic versus the intrafamilial domain, and the therapies that focus on restoring the intrapsychic order is necessary in order to work with clients from many non-Western cultures. Of course, much research is still needed in order to develop more grounded theories and techniques. Shared efforts between researchers and therapists from different cultures and different fields of expertise may promote this process.

A culturally sensitive approach in psychology is very important in this era of globalization, when Western culture is often offered as the ultimate choice for all peoples, regardless of their heritage or culture. Mental health professionals have much knowledge to share; their input can help develop greater understanding of and empathy for the cultures of others and to promote pluralism within globalization.

References

Abd al-Karim, K. (1990). *Al-jothor al-tarikhya li al-sharia'a al-'islamia* [The historical roots of Islamic Sharia'a]. Cairo: Sina lil-Nashr.

Abd El-Gawad, M. S. (1995). Transcultural psychiatry in Egypt. In I. Al-Issa (Ed.), *Handbook of culture and mental illness: An international perspective* (pp. 53–63). Madison, CT: International Universities Press.

Abdu, M. (1947). *Al-Islam wa al-nosrania* [Islam and Christianity]. Cairo: Markaz al-Derasat.

Abraham, N. (1995). Arab Americans. In R. J. Vecoli, J. Galens, A. Sheets, & R. V. Young (Eds.), *Gale encyclopedia of multicultural America* (Vol. 1, pp. 84–98). New York: Gale Research.

Abraham, S. Y. (1983). Detroit's Arab-American community: A survey of diversity and commonality. In S. Y. Abraham & N. Abraham (Eds.), *Arabs in the New World* (pp. 84–108). Detroit: Wayne State University.

Abraham, S. Y., Abraham, N., & Aswad, B. (1983). The Southend: An Arab Muslim working-class community. In S. Y. Abraham & N. Abraham (Eds.), *Arabs in the New World* (pp. 163–184). Detroit: Wayne State University.

Abou-Saleh, M., Younis, Y., & Karim, L. (1998). Anorexia nervosa in an Arab culture. *International Journal of Eating Disorders, 23*(2), 207–212.

Abu-Baker, K. (1985). The impact of cross-cultural contact on the status of Arab women in Israel. In M. Safir, M. T. Mednick, & D. Izraeli (Eds.), *Women's worlds* (pp. 281–296). New York: Praeger.

Abu-Baker, K. (1997). *The impact of immigration on Arab families in South Florida.* Unpublished doctoral dissertation, Nova Southeastern University, Fort Lauderdale, FL.

Abu-Baker, K. (1998). *A rocky road: Arab women as political leaders in Israel* [in Hebrew]. Beit Berl: Institute for Israeli Arab Studies.

Abu-Baker, K. (1999a). Acculturation and reacculturation influence: Multilayer contexts in therapy. *Clinical Psychology Review, 19* (8), 951–967.

Abu-Baker, K. (1999b). The importance of cultural sensitivity and therapist's self-awareness when working with mandatory clients. *Family Process, 38,* 55–67.

Abu-Baker, K. (2002). Arab women, sex, and sexuality: The presence of Arab society and culture in individual and marital therapy among Palestinian women [in Hebrew]. *Hamizrah Hehadash.* Vol. MG, 229–245.

Abu-Baker, K. (2003). "Career women" or "working women"? Change versus stability for young Palestinian women in Israel. *The Journal of Israeli History: Politics, Society, Culture, 21* (1–2), 85–109.

Abu-Baker, K. (in press-a). *Mishpaha u-ribud bahivra haphalestenet betoch yesraeel* [Family and stratification in the Palestinian society inside Israel]. Tel Aviv: Open University.

Abu-Baker, K. (in press-b). Multiple meanings of feminism as an example of multicultural education. Arab feminist as a case study. In P. Peri (Ed.), *Multi-cultural education in Israel* (tentative title). (Hebrew).

Abu-Baker, K., & Dwairy, M. (2003). Cultural norms versus state laws in treating incest: A suggested model for Arab families. *Child Abuse and Neglect, 27,* 109–123.

Abudabbeh, N. (1996). Arab families. In M. McGoldrick, J. Giordano, & J. K. Pearce (Eds.), *Ethnicity and family therapy* (2nd ed., pp. 333–363). New York: Guilford.

Abudabbeh, N., & Nydell, M. K. (1993). Transcultural counseling and Arab Americans. In J. McFadden (Ed.), *Transcultural counseling: Bilateral and international perspectives* (pp. 261–284). Alexandria, VA: American Counseling Association.

Achoui, M. (2003). Ta'adib al-atfal fi al-wasat al-a'ai'li: Waqe'a wa ittijahat [The disciplining of children within the family context: Reality and attitudes]. *Al-tofoolah al-'Arabiah* [Journal on Arab Childhood, Kuwait], *16*(4), 9–38.

Adams, G. R., Shea, J., & Fitch, S. A. (1979). Toward the development of an objective assessment of ego-identity status. *Journal of Youth and Adolescence, 8,* 223–237.

Adler, A. (1959). *The practice and theory of individual psychology.* Totowa, NJ: Littlefield Adams.

Al-Afghani, J. (1968). *Al-'amal al-kamilah li Jamal al-Din al-Afghani* [The complete works of Al-Afghani]. Cairo: Al- Moa'assasa al-Masrya al-A'ama li al-Ta'lif.

Alarcon, R. D., & Foulks, E. F. (1997). Cultural factors and personality disorders. In American Psychiatric Association (1997). *DSM-IV sourcebook* (Vol. 3, pp. 975–982). Washington, DC: American Psychiatric Association.

Al-Dahash, A. B. (1996). *Asaleeb al-'iqab al-mostakhdama fi al-marhala al-ibtidai'yah* [Punishment styles used in elementary schools]. Unpublished master's thesis, Department of Education, King Fahd University, Dhahran, Saudi Arabia.

Al-Haj, M. (1989). Social research on family lifestyle among Arabs in Israel. *Journal of Comparative Family Studies, 20*(2), 175–195.

Al-Issa, I. (1989). Psychiatry in Algeria. *Psychiatric Bulletin, 13,* 240–245.

Al-Issa, I. (1995). The illusion of reality or the reality of illusion: Hallucination and culture. *British Journal of Psychiatry, 166,* 368–373.

Al-Jabiri, M. A. (1991a). *Takween al-'aql al-'arabi* [Formation of Arab thought]. Beirut: Al-Markaz al-Thaqafi al-'Arabi.

Al-Jabiri, M. A. (1991b). *Al-'aql as-siyasi al-'arabi* [Arab political thought]. Beirut: Al-Markaz al-Thaqafi al-'Arabi.

Al Jabiri, M. A. (2002). *Al-'aql al-akhlaqi al-'arabi* [Arab moral thought]. Beirut: Al-Markaz al-Thaqafi al-'Arabi.

Al-Khawaja, M. Y. (1999). Al-shabab al-'arabi [Arab youth]. In K. Zakariya (Ed.), *Derasat fi al-mojtama'a al-'arabi* [Studies of Arab society] (pp. 255–304). Damascus: Al-Ahali.

Al-Kittani, F. (2000). *Al-ittijahat al-walideyah fi al-tanshia'a al-ijtima'ayah* [Parents' approaches in socialization]. Amman: Dar Al-Shorooq.

Alldredge, E., E. (1984). Child-rearing practices in the homes of Arab immigrants: A study of ethnic persistence (Doctoral dissertation, Michigan State University, 1984). *Dissertation Abstract International, 45*(12), p. 3753.

Al-Mahroos, F. (2001, October). Rasd thaherat soo'a al-moa'amalah fil Bahrain [Observation on abuse in Bahrain]. Abstract of the conference on child abuse, Bahraini Society for Child Development, Bahrain, October, 20–22.

Al-Sabaie, A. (1989). Psychiatry in Saudi Arabia: cultural perspectives. *Transcultural Psychiatric Research Review, 26,* 245–262.

Al-Shqerat, M. A., & Al-Masri, A. N. (2001). Al-isaa'a al-laftheyah ded al-atfal [Verbal abuse against children]. *Majallat al-tofoolah al-'arabiah* [Journal of Arab Childhood], *2*(7), 33–45.

Al-Tahtawi, R. R. (1973). *Al-'amal al-kamilah li Rifa'ah al-Tahtawi* [The complete works of Al-Tahtawi]. Beirut: Al-Moa'assasa al-'Arabia li al-Derasat wa al-Nashr.

American Psychiatric Association (APA). (1997). *DSM-IV sourcebook* (Vol. 3). Washington, DC: American Psychiatric Association.

'Authman, W. (1999). Al-'a'aila al-'arabia [The Arab family]. In K. Zakariya (Ed.), *Derasat fi al-mojtama'a al-'arabi* [Studies of Arab society] (pp. 177–218). Damascus: Al-Ahali.

Arab American Institute (AAI). (2005). Arab American demographics. Retrieved October 28, 2005, from https://aaiusa.org/demographics.htm

Baasher, T. (1962). Some aspects of the history of the treatment of mental disorders in the Sudan. *Sudan Medical Journal, 1,* 44.

Barakat, H. (1993). *The Arab world: Society, culture, and state.* Los Angeles: University of California Press.

Barakat, H. (2000). *Al-mojtama'a al-'arabi fi al-qarn al-'ashrin* [Arab society in the twentieth century]. Beirut: Markaz Derasat al-Wehda al-'Arabia.

Barazangi, N. H. (1996). Parents and youth: Perceiving and practicing Islam in North America. In B. C. Aswad & B. Bilgé (Eds.), *Family and gender among American Muslims: Issues facing Middle Eastern immigrants and their descendants* (pp. 129–142). Philadelphia: Temple University Press.

Baron, A. E., Manson, S. M., & Ackerson, L. M. (1990). Depressive symptomatology in older American Indians with chronic disease: Some psychometric considerations. In C. Attkinsson & J. Zich (Eds.), *Screening for depression in primary care* (pp. 217–231). New York: Routledge.

Beck, A. T. (1967). *Depression: Clinical experimental, and theoretical aspects.* New York: Hoebet. (Republished as *Depression: Causes and treatment.* Philadelphia: University of Pennsylvania Press, 1972)

Bennion, L., & Adams, G. R. (1986). A revision of the extended version of the objective measure of ego identity status: An identity instrument for use with late adolescents. *Journal of Adolescent Research, 1,* 183–198.

Berg-Cross, L., & Chinen, R. T. (1995). Multicultural training models and person-in-culture interview. In J. G. Ponterotto, J. M. Casas, L. A. Suzuki, & C. M. Alexander (Eds.), *Handbook of multicultural counseling* (pp. 333–356). Thousand Oaks, CA: Sage.

Bigner, J. J. (1994). *Individual and family development: A life-span interdisciplinary approach.* Englewood Cliffs, NJ: Prentice Hall.

Bilgé, B., & Aswad, B. C. (1996). Introduction. In B. C. Aswad & B. Bilgé (Eds.),

Family and gender among American Muslims: Issues facing Middle Eastern immigrants and their descendants (pp. 1–16). Philadelphia: Temple University Press.

Blos, P. (1967). The second individuation process of adolescence. *Psychoanalytic Studies of the Child, 22,* 162–186.

Bonnie, M., & Hasan, N. T. (2004). Arab American persons' reported experiences of discrimination and mental health: The mediating role of personal control. *Journal of Counseling Psychology, 51*(4). 418–426.

Bresler, D. (1984). Mind-controlled analgesia: The inner way to pain control. In A. A. Sheikh (Ed.), *Imagination and healing: Imagery and human development series* (pp. 211–230). New York: Baywood.

Budman, C. L., Lipson, J. G., & Meleis, A. I. (1992). The cultural consultant in mental health care: The case of an Arab adolescent. *American Journal of Orthopsychiatry, 62*(3), 359–370.

Cainkar, L. (1996). Immigrant Palestinian women evaluate their lives. In B. C. Aswad & B. Bilgé (Eds.), *Family and gender among American Muslims: Issues facing Middle Eastern immigrants and their descendants* (pp. 85–105). Philadelphia: Temple University Press.

Central Intelligence Agency Web (November, 2003): www.reference-guides.com/cia_world_factbook.

Chenail, R. J., & Morrris, G. H. (1995). The talk of the clinic: An introduction. In G. H. Morris & R. J. Chenail (Eds.), *The talk of the clinic: Explorations in the analysis of medical and therapeutic discourse* (pp. 1–15). Hillsdale, NJ: Lawrence Earlbaum.

Conklin, N. F., & Faires, N. (1987). "Colored" and Catholic: The Lebanese in Birmingham, Alabama. In E. J. Hooglund (Ed.), *Crossing the waters: Arabic-speaking immigrants to the United States before 1940* (pp. 69–84). Washington, DC: Smithsonian Institution Press.

Cooper, J. E., Jablensky, A., & Sartorius, N. (1990). WHO collaborative studies on acute psychosis using the SCAAPS schedule. In C. N. Stefanis (Ed.), *Psychiatry: A worldwide perspective.* New York: Elsevier Science.

Costantino, G., Malgady, R., & Vasquez, C. (1981). A comparison of the Murray-TAT and the new thematic apperception test for urban Hispanic children. *Hispanic Journal of Behavioral Science, 3,* 291–300.

Dana, R. H. (1993). *Multicultural assessment perspectives for professional psychology.* Boston: Allyn & Bacon.

Dasen, P. R. (1977). *Piagetian psychology: Cross-cultural contributions.* New York: Gardner Press.

Dasen, P. R., & Heron, A. (1981). Cross-cultural tests of Piaget's theory. In H. C. Triandis & A. Heron (Eds.), *Handbook of cross-cultural psychology: Vol. 4. Developmental psychology.* Newton, MA: Allyn & Bacon.

deMause, L. (1974). The evolution of childhood. In L. deMause (Ed.), *The history of childhood.* New York: Harper & Row.

De Vos, G., & Boyer, L. B. (1989). *Symbolic analysis cross-culturally: The Rorschach Test.* Berkeley: University of California Press.

Donaldson, B. A. (1981). The evil eye in Iran. In A. Dundes (Ed.), *The evil eye: A folklore casebook* (pp. 66–77). New York: Garland.

Dreikurs, R. (1949). The four goals of children's misbehavior. *Nervous Child, 6,* 3–11.

Dube, E. F. (1982). Literacy, cultural familiarity, and intelligence as determinants of story recall. In U. Neisser (Ed.), *Memory observed: Remembering in natural contexts.* San Francisco: W. H. Freeman.

Dwairy, M. (1997a). A biopsychosocial model of metaphor therapy with holistic cultures. *Clinical Psychology Review, 17*(7), 719–732.

Dwairy, M. (1997b). Addressing the repressed needs of the Arabic client. *Cultural Diversity and Mental Health, 3*(1), 1–12.

Dwairy, M. (1997c). *Personality, culture, and Arabic society* [in Arabic]. Jerusalem: Al-Noor.

Dwairy, M. (1998a). *Cross-cultural counseling: The Arab-Palestinian case.* New York: Haworth Press.

Dwairy, M. (1998b). Mental health in the Arab world. In A. S. Bellack & M. Hersen (Eds.), *Comprehensive clinical psychology: Sociocultural and individual differences* (Vol. 10, pp. 313–324). New York: Pergamon Press.

Dwairy, M. (Ed.). (1999a). Cross-cultural psychotherapy [Special issue]. *Clinical Psychology Review, 19*(8).

Dwairy, M. (1999b). Toward psycho-cultural approach in Middle Eastern societies. *Clinical Psychology Review, 19*(8), 909–916.

Dwairy, M. (2001). Therapeutic use of the physical environment: Talking about a significant object. *Journal of Clinical Activities, Assignments and Handouts in Psychotherapy Practice: Innovations in resources for treatment and intervention, 1*(1), pp. 61–71.

Dwairy, M. (2002a). Foundations of psychosocial dynamic personality theory of collective people. *Clinical Psychology Review, 22,* 343–360.

Dwairy, M. (2002b). Psychotherapy in competition with culture: A case study of an Arabic woman. *Clinical Case Studies, 1*(3), 254–267.

Dwairy, M. (2003). Components of physical environment as metaphors in therapy. *Annals of American Psychotherapy Association, 6*(1), 34–40.

Dwairy, M. (2004a). Culturally sensitive education: Adapting self-oriented assertiveness training to collective minorities. *Journal of Social Issues, 60*(2), 423–436.

Dwairy, M. (2004b). Individuation among Bedouin versus urban Arab adolescents: National, ethnic and gender differences. *Cultural Diversity and Ethnic Minority Psychology, 10*(4), 340–350.

Dwairy, M. (2004c). Internal-structural validity of Objective Measure of Ego-Identity Status among Arab adolescents. *Identity: An International Journal of Theory and Research, 4*(2), 133–144.

Dwairy, M. (2004d). Parenting styles and psychological adjustment of Arab adolescents. *Transcultural Psychiatry, 41*(2), 233–252.

Dwairy, M. (2004e). Parenting styles and mental health of Arab gifted adolescents. *Gifted Child Quarterly, 48*(4), 275–286.

Dwairy, M., & Abu Baker, K. (1992, December). The use of stories in psychotherapy [in Arabic]. *Al-Thaqafa* [Education], *1,* 34–37.

Dwairy, M., Achoui, M., Abouserie, R., & Farah, A. (in press). Parenting styles, individuation, and mental health of Arab adolescents: A third cross-regional research study. *Journal of Cross-Cultural Psychology.*

Dwairy, M., & Menshar, K. E. (in press). Parenting style, individuation, and mental health of Egyptian adolescents. *Journal of Adolescence.*

Dwairy, M., & Van Sickle, T. (1996) Western psychotherapy in traditional Arabic societies. *Clinical Psychology Review, 16*(3), 231–249.

Eisenbruch, M. (1991). From post-traumatic stress disorder to cultural bereavement: Diagnosis of Southeast Asian refugees. *Social Science Medicine, 33,* 673–680.

Eisenlohr, C. J. (1996). Adolescent Arab girls in an American high school. In B. C. Aswad & B. Bilgé (Eds.), *Family and gender among American Muslims: Issues facing Middle Eastern immigrants and their descendants* (pp. 250–270). Philadelphia: Temple University Press.

El-Badry, S. (1994, January). The Arab-American market. *American Demographics, 16,* 22–30.

El-Islam, M. F. (1979). A better outlook for schizophrenics living in extended families. *British Journal of Psychiatry, 135,* 343.

El-Islam, M. F. (1982). Arabic cultural psychiatry. *Transcultural Psychiatric Research Review, 19,* 5–24.

Ellis, A. (1962). *Reason and emotion in psychotherapy.* Secaucus, NJ: Citadel.

El-Sarrag, M. E. (1968). Psychiatry in the Northern Sudan: A study in comparative psychiatry. *British Journal of Psychiatry, 114,* 946–948.

Erickson, C. D., & Al-Tamimi, N. R. (2001). Providing mental health services to Arab Americans: Recommendations and considerations. *Cultural Diversity and Ethnic Minority Psychology, 7*(4), 308–327.

Erikson, E. H. (1950). *Childhood and society.* New York: Norton.

Ewen, R. B. (2003). *An introduction to theories of personality.* London: Lawrence Erlbaum.

Fabrega, H., Swartz, J. D., & Wallace, C. A. (1968). Ethnic differences in psychopathology, II: Specific differences with emphasis on a Mexican American group. *Psychiatry Research, 6,* 221–235.

Fa'ik, A. (1994). Issues of identity: In theater of immigrant community. In E. McCarus (Ed.), *The development of Arab-American identity* (pp. 107–118). Ann Arbor: University of Michigan Press.

Fargness, P. (1996). The Arab world: The family as fortress. In A. Burguière, C. Klapish-Zuber, M. Sogalen, & F. Zonabend (Eds.), *A history of the family: Vol. 2. The impact of modernity* (pp. 339–374). Cambridge, MA: Belknap Press.

Fernando, S. (1988). *Race and culture in psychiatry.* London: Croom Helm.

Fisek, G. O., & Kagitcibasi, C. (1999). Multiculturalism and psychotherapy: The Turkish case. In P. B. Pedersen (Ed.), *Multiculturalism as a fourth force.* (pp. 75–92), Philadelphia: Brunner/Mazel.

Fiske, A. P. (1990). *Structure of social life.* New York: Free Press.

Fiske, A. P. (1992). The four elementary forms of sociality: Framework for a unified theory of social relations. *Psychology Review, 99,* 689–723.

Frankl, V. E. (1959). *Man's search for meaning.* New York: Pocket Books. (Original work published 1946)

Freire, P. (1994). *Pedagogy of hope: Reliving pedagogy of the oppressed..* New York: Continuum. (Original work published 1992)

Freire, P. (1995). *Pedagogy of the oppressed* (revised 20th anniversary ed.). New York: Continuum. (Original work published 1970)

Freud, S. (1964a). *The interpretation of dreams.* In J. Strachey (Ed. & Trans.), *The standard edition of the complete psychological works of Sigmund Freud* (Vol. 4.). London: Hogarth Press. (Original work published 1900)

Freud, S. (1964b). An outline of psychoanalysis. In J. Strachey (Ed. & Trans.), *The standard edition of the complete psychological works of Sigmund Freud* (Vol. 23). London: Hogarth Press. (Original work published 1940)

Fromm, E. (1941). *Escape from freedom.* New York: Henry Holt.

Fromm, E. (1976). *To have or to be?* New York: Harper & Row.

Garcia, M., & Marks, G. (1989). Depressed symptomatology among Mexican-American adults: An examination of the CES-D scale. *Psychiatry Research, 27,* 137–148.

Gavazzi, S. M., & Sabatelli, R. M. (1987, November). *Assessing levels of individuation through multigenerational interconnectedness.* Paper presented at the 49th Annual Conference of the National Council of Family Relations, Atlanta.

Gavazzi, S. M., & Sabatelli, R. M. (1988). *Multigenerational interconnectedness and family involvement: Assessing levels of individuation in adolescence and early adulthood.* Paper presented at the National Council on Family Relations Conference, Philadelphia, PA.

Ghanem, A. (2001). *The Palestinian-Arab minority in Israel, 1948–2000.* Albany: State University of New York Press.

Good, B. J., & Good, M. J. (1982). Toward a meaning-centered analysis of popular illness: Categories "fright illness" and "heart distress" in Iran. In A. J. Marsella & G. M. White (Eds.), *Cultural conceptions of mental health and therapy* (pp. 141–166). Boston: D. Reidel.

Goodwin, R., & Giles, S. (2004). Social support provision and cultural values in Indonesia and Britain. *Journal of Cross-Cultural Psychology, 34*(2): 240–245.

Gorkin, M., Masalha, S., & Yatziv, G. (1985). Psychotherapy of Israeli-Arab patients: Some cultural consideration. *The Journal of Psychoanalytic Anthropology, 8*(4), 215–230.

Grieger, I., & Ponterotto, J. G. (1995). A framework for assessment in multicultural counseling. In J. G. Ponterotto, J. M. Casas, L. A. Suzuki, & C. M. Alexander (Eds.), *Handbook of multicultural counseling* (pp. 357–374). Thousand Oaks, CA: Sage Publications.

Grinberg, L., & Grinberg, R. (1989). *Psychoanalytic perspectives on migration and exile.* (N. Festinger, Trans.). New Haven, CT: Yale University Press. (Original work published 1984)

Guarnaccia, P. J., Good, B. J., & Kleinman, A. (1990). A critical review of epidemiological studies of Puerto Rican mental health. *American Journal of Psychiatry, 147,* 1449–1456.

Haddad, Y. (1983). Arab Muslims and Islamic institutions in America: Adaptation and reform. In S. Y. Abraham & N. Abraham (Eds.), *Arabs in the New World* (pp. 64–81). Detroit: Wayne State University.

Halaby, R. J. (1987). Dr. Michael Shadid and the debate over identity in the Syrian World. In E. J. Hooglund (Ed.), *Crossing the waters: Arabic-speaking immigrants to the United States before 1940* (pp. 37–54). Washington, DC: Smithsonian Institution Press.

Hall, G. S. (1891). The concepts of children's minds on entering school. *Pedagogical Seminary, 1,* 139–173.

Hall, G. S. (1904). *Adolescence.* New York: Appleton-Century-Crofts.

Hare-Mustin, R. T., & Marecek, J. (1988). The meaning of difference. *American Psychologist, 43*(6), 455–464.

Harfouche, J. K. (1981). The evil eye and infant health in Lebanon. In A. Dundes (Ed.), *The evil eye: A folklore casebook* (pp. 86–106). New York: Garland.

Hatab, Z., & Makki, A. (1978). *Al-solta el-abawia wa al-shabab* [Parental authority and youth]. Beirut: Maʿhad al-Inmaʾa al-ʿArabi.

Heilman, S. C., & Witztum, E. (1997). Value-sensitive therapy: Learning from Ultra-Orthodox patients. *American Journal of Psychotherapy, 51*(4), 522–541.

Hofstede, G. (1980). *Culture's consequences: International differences in work-related values.* Beverly Hills, CA: Sage.

Hofstede, G. (1986). Cultural differences in teaching and learning. *International Journal of Intercultural Relations, 10*(3): 301–320.

Hofstede, G. (1991). *Cultures and organizations: Software of the mind.* London: McGraw-Hill.

Hourani, A. (1983). *Arabic thought in the liberal age.* London: Cambridge University Press.

Hourani, A. (1991). *A history of the Arab peoples.* New York: Warner Books.

Ibish, I. (2003). *Report on hate crimes and discrimination against Arab Americans.* Washington, DC: American-Arab Anti-Discrimination Committee.

Ibrahim, F. A., & Khan, H. (1987). Assessment of worldviews. *Psychological Reports, 60,* 163–176.

Ibrahim, F. A., Ohnishi, H., & Wilson, R. P. (1994). Career assessment in a culturally diverse society. *Journal of Career Assessment, 2,* 276–288.

Institute of Islamic Information and Education. (2005). Muslim population statistics. Retrieved December 6, 2005, from http://www.iiie.net/1/content/view/130/44/.

Ivey, A., Ivey, M. B., & Simek-Morgan, L. (1997). *Counseling and psychotherapy: A multicultural perspective* (4th ed.). Boston: Allyn & Bacon.

Ivey, A., Simek-Morgan, L., D'Andrea, M., & Ivey, M. B. (2001). *Counseling and psychotherapy: A multicultural perspective* (5th ed.). New York: Pearson Education.

Jackson, M. (1997). Counseling Arab Americans. In C. Lee (Ed.), *Multicultural issues in counseling: New approaches to diversity* (2nd ed., pp 333–349). Alexandria, VA: American Counseling Association.

Jamil, H., Hakim-Larson, J., Farrag, M., Kafaji, T., Duqum, I., & Jamil, L. H. (2002). A retrospective study of Arab American mental health clients: Trauma and the Iraqi refugees. *American Journal of Orthopsychiatry, 72*(3), 355–361.

Joseph, S. (Ed.). (1999). *Intimate selving: Self, gender and identity in Arab families.* Syracuse, NY: Syracuse University Press.

Joseph, S. (Ed.). (2000). *Gender and citizenship in the Middle East.* Syracuse, NY: Syracuse University Press.

Jung, C. G. (1953). *Collected works.* London: Routledge & Kegan Paul.

Jung, C. G. (1959). *The undiscovered self.* New York: American Library.

Kagitcibasi, C. (1996). The autonomous-relational self: A new synthesis. *European Psychologist, 1*(3), 180–186.

Kayal, P. M. (1983). Arab Christians in the United States. In S. Y. Abraham & N. Abraham (Eds.), *Arabs in the New World* (pp. 44–63). Detroit: Wayne State University.

Kearins, J. M. (1981). Visual-spatial memory in Australian aboriginal children of desert regions. *Cognitive Psychology, 13,* 434–460.

Keith, J. (1985). Age in anthropological research. In R. H. Binstock & E. Shanus (Eds.), *Handbook of aging and the social sciences* (2nd ed.). New York: Van Nostrand Reinhold.

Khalaf, S. (1987). The background and causes of Lebanese/Syrian immigration to the United States before World War I. In E. J. Hooglund (Ed.), *Crossing the waters: Arabic-speaking immigrants to the United States before 1940* (pp. 17–35). Washington, DC: Smithsonian Institution Press.

Kira, I. A. (1999, August). *Type III trauma and the Iraqi refugees' traumatic experiences.* Paper presented at the 107th annual convention of the American Psychological Association, Boston.

Kleinman, A. (1986). *Social origins of distress and disease.* New Haven, CT: Yale University Press.

Kopp, R. R. (1995). *Metaphor therapy: Using client-generated metaphors in psychotherapy.* New York: Brunner/Mazel.

Kroger, J. (1993). Ego identity: An overview. In J. Kroger (Ed.), *Discussions on ego identity* (pp. 1–20). Hillsdale, NJ: Lawrence Erlbaum.

Kuo, W. (1984). Prevalence of depression among Asian Americans. *Journal of Nervous and Mental Disease, 172,* 449–457.

Laing, R. D. (1959). *The divided self.* Baltimore: Penguin.

Landrine, H. (1992). Clinical implications of cultural difference. The referential versus indexical self. *Clinical Psychology Review, 12,* 401–415.

Lazarus, A. A. (2000). Multimodal therapy. In R. J. Corsini & D. Wedding (Eds.), *Current psychotherapies* (6th ed., pp. 340–374). Itasca, IL: Peacock.

Levine, R. V., Norenzayan, A., & Philbrick, K. (2001). Cross-cultural differences in helping strangers. *Journal of Cross-Cultural Psychology, 32*(5), 543–560.

Levitt, E. E., & Truumaa, A. (1972). *The Rorschach technique with children and adolescents: Application and norms.* New York: Grune & Stratton.

Lin, K. M., & Kleinman, A. M. (1988). Psychopathology and clinical course of schizophrenia: A cross-cultural perspective. *Schizophrenia Bulletin, 14,* 555–567.

Lonner, W. J. (1990). An overview of cross-cultural testing and assessment. In R. W. Brislin (Ed.), *Applied cross-cultural psychology* (pp. 56–76). London: Sage.

Lovel, E. K. (1983). Islam in the United States: Past and present. In E. H. Waught, B. Abu-Laban, & R. B. Qurashi (Eds.), *The Muslim community in North American* (pp. 93–110). Edmonton: University of Alberta Press.

Mahler, M., Bergman, A., & Pine, F. (1975). *The psychological birth of the infant: Symbiosis and individuation.* New York: Basic Books.

Manson, S. M. (1997). Cultural considerations in the diagnosis of mood disorders. In American Psychiatric Association (Ed.), *DSM-IV sourcebook* (Vol. 3, pp. 317–391). Washington, DC: Author.

Manson, S. M., Ackerson, L. M., & Dick, R. W. (1990). Depressive symptoms among American Indian adolescents: Psychometric characteristics of the Center for Epidemiologic Studies Depression Scale (CES-D). *Psychological Assessment, 2,* 231–237.

Markus, H. R., & Kitayama, S. (1998). The cultural psychology of personality. *Journal of Cross-Cultural Psychology and Research, 29*(1), 63–87.

Marsella, A. J. (1978). Thoughts on cross-cultural studies on epidemiology of depression. *Culture, Medicine, and Psychiatry, 2,* 343–357.

May, R. (1977). *The meaning of anxiety.* New York: Norton. (Original work published 1950)

McCarus, E. (Ed.). (1994). *The development of Arab-American identity.* Ann Arbor: University of Michigan Press.

Meleis, A. I. (1981, June). The Arab American in the health care system. *American Journal of Nursing,* 1180–1183.

Meleis, A. I., & La Fever, C. W. (1984). The Arab American and psychiatric care. *Perspectives in Psychiatric Care, 22*(2), 72–86.

Mernissi, F. (1992). *The veil and the male elite: A feminist interpretation of women's rights in Islam.* London: Perseus Books.

Mernissi, F. (1993). *Women and Islam: An historical and theological enquiry.* New York: Kali for Women.

Monte, C. F., & Sollod, R. N. (2003). *Beneath the mask: An introduction to theories of personality* (7th ed.). Danvers, MA: John Wiley.

Moradi, B., & Hasan, N. T. (2004). Arab American Persons' reported experiences of discrimination and mental health: The mediating role of personal control. *Journal of Counseling Psychology, 51*(4), 418–428.

Murphy, H. B. M. (1982). *Comparative psychiatry: The international and intercultural distribution of mental illness.* New York: Springer-Verlag..

Murphy, H. B. M., & Ramman, A. C. (1971). The chronicity of schizophrenia in indigenous tropical people: results of a 12-years follow-up on Mauritius. *British Journal of Psychiatry, 118,* 489–497

Naff, A. (1983). Arabs in America: A historical overview. In S. Y. Abraham & N. Abraham (Eds.), *Arabs in the New World* (pp. 8–29). Detroit: Wayne State University, Center for Urban Studies.

Naff, A. (1985). *Becoming American: The early Arab immigrant experience.* Carbondale, IL: Southern Illinois University Press.

Najati, M. A. (2001). *Al-Qur'an wa 'alm al-nafs* [The Qu'ran and psychology]. Cairo: Dar Al-Shorouk.

Nasser, M. (1986). Comparative study of prevalence of abnormal eating attitudes among Arab female students of both London and Cairo universities. *Psychological Medicine, 16,* 621–625.

Nasser, M. (1988). Eating disorders: The cultural dimension. *Social Psychiatry and Psychiatric Epidemiology, 23,* 184–187.

Ndetei, D. M., & Vadher, A. (1984). A cross-cultural study of the frequencies of Schneider's first rank symptoms of schizophrenia. *Acta Psychiatry Scandinavia, 70,* 540–544.

Nobles, A., & Sciarra, D. T. (2000). Cultural determinants in the treatment of Arab

Americans: A primer for mainstream therapists. *American Journal of Orthopsychiatry, 70*(2), 182–191.

Noor El-Deen, M. A. (2000). *Al-tamweh fi al-mojtamaʿa al-ʿarabi al-soltawi* [Camouflage in the authoritarian Arab society]. Casablanca, Morocco: Al-Markaz al-Thaqafi al-ʿArabi.

Noorzoy, M. S. (1983). Islamic laws on *riba* (interest) and their full economic implications. In E. H. Waugh, B. Abu-Laban, & R. B. Qureshi (Eds.), *The Muslim community in North America* (pp. 50–71). Edmonton: University of Alberta Press.

Okasha, A. (1993). Psychiatry in Egypt. *Psychiatric Bulletin, 17,* 548–551.

Okasha, A. (1999). Mental health in the Middle East: An Egyptian perspective. *Clinical Psychology Review, 19*(8), 917–933.

Okasha, A., Saad, A., Khalil, A. H., Seif El Dawla, A., & Yehia, N. (1994). Phenomenology of obsessive-compulsive disorder: A transcultural study. *Comprehensive Psychiatry, 35*(3), 191–197.

Okasha, A., Seif El Dawla, A., Khalil, A. H., & Saad, A. (1993). Presentation of acute psychosis in an Egyptian sample: A transcultural comparison. *Comprehensive Psychiatry, 34*(1), 4–9.

Panorama [newspaper]. (2003, August 29). Taibi, Israel.

Patai, R. (1983). *The Arab mind.* New York: Charles Scribner's Sons.

Patai, R. (2002). *The Arab mind.* New York: Hatherleigh Press.

Pedersen, P. B. (1990). The multicultural perspective as a fourth force in psychology. *Journal of Counseling and Development, 70,* 3–14.

Pedersen, P. B. (1999). Culture-centered interventions as a fourth dimension of psychology. In P. B. Pedersen (Ed.), *Multiculturalism as a fourth force* (pp. 3–18). Philadelphia: Brunner/Mazel.

Perls, F. (1976). *The Gestalt approach and eyewitness to therapy.* New York: Bantam. (Original work published 1973)

Piaget, J. (1950). *The psychology of intelligence.* San Diego, CA: Harcourt Brace Jovanovich.

Piaget, J. (1970). Piaget's theory. In P. H. Mussen (Ed.), *Carmichael's manual of child psychology* (Vol. 1). New York: Wiley.

Pipes, D., & Duran, K. (2002, August/September). Faces of American Islam [:Muslim Immigration]. http:// www.danielpipes.org/article/441.

Pristin, T., & Dart, J. (1991, January 20). Islam in America: Muslims as a growing force in U.S. *Los Angeles Times*, p. A1.

Qasem, F. S., Mustafa, A. A., Kazem, N. A., & Shah, N. M. (1998). Attitude of Kuwaiti parents toward physical punishment of children. *Child Abuse and Neglect, 22,* 1189–1202.

Racy, J. (1970). Psychiatry in the Arab East. *Acta Psychiatrica Scandinavica, 221,* 160–171.

Racy, J. (1977). Psychiatry in the Arab East. In C. L. Brown & N. Itzkowitz (Eds.), *Psychological dimensions of Near Eastern studies* (pp. 279–329). Princeton, NJ: Darwin Press.

Radloff, L. S. (1977). The CES-D scale: A self-report depression scale for research in the general population. *Applied Psychological Measurement, 1,* 385–401.

Ridley, C. R., & Lingle, D. W. (1996). Cultural empathy in multicultural counseling: A multidimensional process model. In P. B. Pedersen, J. G. Draguns, W. J. Lonner, & J. E. Trimble (Eds.), *Counseling across cultures* (4th ed., pp. 21–46). Thousand Oaks, CA: Sage.

Rogers, C. R. (1951). *Client-centered therapy.* Boston: Houghton Mifflin.

Rogers, C. R. (1961). *On becoming a person..* Boston: Houghton Mifflin.

Rosaldo, M. (1984). Toward an anthropology of self and feeling. In R. A. Shweder & R. A. LeVine (Eds.), *Culture theory: Essays on mind, self, and emotion* (pp. 137–157). Cambridge MA: Cambridge University Press.

Russell, G. F. M. (1993). Social psychiatry of eating disorders. In D. Bhugra & J. Leff (Eds.), *Modern trends in psychological medicine* (pp. 131–164). London: Butterworths.

Saif El-Deen, A. (2001, October). Soo'a al-moa'amalah wa ihmal al-atfal [Abuse and neglect of children]. Abstract of the conference on child abuse, Bahrain, October, 20–22.

Sampson, E. E. (1988). The debate on individualism. *American Psychologist, 43*(1), 15–22.

Sampson, E. E. (1989). The challenge of social change for psychology: Globalization and psychology's theory of the person. *American Psychologist, 44*, 914–921.

Scott, N. E., & Borodovsky, L. (1990). Effective use of cultural role taking. *Professional Psychology: Research and Practice, 21*, 167–170.

Shaffer, D. R. (1996). *Developmental psychology: Childhood and adolescence.* New York: Brooks/Cole.

Simon, G. E., & Von Korff, M. (1991). Somatization and psychiatric disorder in the NIMH epidemiologic catchment area study. *American Journal of Psychiatry, 148*, 1494–1500.

Simon, J. P. (1996). Lebanese families. In M. McGoldrick, J. Giordano, & J. K. Pearce (Eds.), *Ethnicity and family therapy* (2nd ed., pp. 364–375). New York: Guilford Press.

Simon, R. C., & Hughes, C. C. (1993). Culture-bound syndromes. In A. C. Gaw (Ed.), *Culture, ethnicity, and mental illness* (pp. 75–100). Washington, DC: American Psychiatric Press.

Singelis, T. M. (1994). The measurement of independent and interdependent self-construals. *Personality and Social Psychology Bulletin, 20*, 580–591.

Stockton, R. (1994). Ethnic archetypes and the Arab image. In E. McCarus (Ed.), *The development of Arab-American identity* (pp. 119–153). Ann Arbor: University of Michigan Press.

Sue, D. W. (1978). World views and counseling. *Personnel and Guidance Journal, 56*(8), 458–463.

Sue, D. W., & Sue, D. (1990). *Counseling the culturally different: Theory and practice.* New York: Wiley.

Suleiman, M. W. (1987). Early Arab-American: The search for identity. In E. J. Hooglund (Ed.), *Crossing the waters: Arabic-speaking immigrants to the United States before 1940* (pp. 17–35). Washington, DC: Smithsonian Institution Press.

Suleiman, M. W., (1988). *Arabs in the mind of America.* Brattleboro, VT: Amana Books.

Swanson, J. C. (1996). Ethnicity, marriage, and role conflict: The dilemma of a second-generation Arab-American. In B. C. Aswad & B. Bilgé (Eds.), *Family and gender among American Muslims: Issues facing Middle Eastern immigrants and their descendants* (pp. 1–16). Philadelphia: Temple University Press.

Thompson, C. (1949). The Thompson modification of the Thematic Apperception Test. *Psychological Assessment, 6*(3), 212–217.

Timimi, S. B. (1995). Adolescence in immigrant Arab families. *Psychotherapy, 32,* 141–149.

Triandis, H. C. (1990). Theoretical concepts that are applied to the analysis of ethnocentrism. In R. W. Brislin (Ed.), *Applied cross-cultural psychology* (pp. 34–55). London: Sage.

Triandis, H. C. (1995). *Individualism and collectivism.* San Francisco: Westview Press.

Tuncer, C. (1995). Mental health in an Islamic-Mediterranean culture: Turkey. In I. Al-Issa (Ed.). *Handbook of Culture and mental illness: An international perspective* (pp. 53–63). Madison, CT: International Universities Press.

Umlil, A. (1985). *Al-Islahiya wa al-dawla al-wataniya* [Reform and the nation-state]. Casablanca: Al-Markes al-Thaqafi al-ʿArabi.

United Nations Development Programme (UNDP). (2002). Arab human development report 2002: Creating opportunity for future generations. New York: Author.

Vygotsky, I. S. (1962). *Thought and language.* Cambridge, MA: MIT Press. (Original work published 1934)

Vygotsky, I. S. (1978). *Mind in society: The development of higher mental processes* (M. Cole, V. John-Steiner, S. Scribner, & E. Souberman, Eds.). Cambridge, MA: Harvard University Press. (Original work published 1930, 1933, 1935)

Waugh, E. H., Abu-Laban, B., & Qureshi, R. B. (Eds.). (1983). *The Muslim community in North America.* Edmonton: University of Alberta Press.

Waxler, N. (1977). Is outcome for schizophrenia better in non-industrialized societies? The case of Sri-Lanka. *Journal of Nervous and Mental Disease, 167,* 144–158.

Winnicott, D. (1953). Transitional objects and transitional phenomena. *International Journal of Psychoanalysis, 34*(2), 89–97.

Witztum, E., & Goodman, Y. (2003). *Hafra'a, sopur, tipol: hita'arvut astrateget narativit regishat tarbut baokhlusiah haredit* [Disorder, story, treatment: Strategic narrative and culturally sensitive intervention with Orthodox Jews]. In E. Leshem, & D. Stryar (Eds.), *Shonut tarbotit keitgar leshirute inosh* [Cultural diversity as challenge to human services] (pp. 275–309). Jerusalem: Magins, Hebrew University Press.

World Health Organization. (1973). *The international pilot study of schizophrenia.* Geneva: Author.

World Health Organization. (1979). *Schizophrenia: An international follow-up.* New York: John Wiley.

Ying, Y. (1988). Depressive symptomatology among Chinese-Americans as measured by the CES-D. *Journal of Clinical Psychology, 44,* 739–746.

Yusooff, F. (2003, December 13–18). *Self-blame among abused wives.* Paper presented at the Middle-East/North Africa Regional Conference of Psychology, organized by IUPsyS, IACCP, and IAAP in Dubai, United Arab Emirates.

Zakariya, K. (1999). *Derasat fi al-mojtamaʿa al-ʿarabi* [Studies of Arab society]. Damascus: Al-Ahali.

Zogby, J. (1990). *Arab American today: A demographic profile of Arab Americans.* Washington, DC: Arab American Institute.

Zogby, J. (2001, October). *Arab American attitudes and the September 11 attacks.* Retrieved from http://www.aaiusa.org/PDF/attitudes.pdf; www.aaiusa.org/demographics. htm

Index

Abd al-Karim, K., 12
Abd El-Gawad, M. S., 86, 87
Abdu, M., 20
Abou-Saleh, M., 91, 92
Abouserie, R., 27
Abraham, N., 31, 33–34, 39–41
Abraham, S. Y., 29, 33–34, 42
Abu-Baker, K., 13, 29–43, 32, 118, 120–137, 121, 122, 124, 128, 131, 137n
Abudabbeh, N., 29, 125, 130–131
Abu-Laban, B., 42
Acculturation, 14–15, 32
  of children versus parents, 133–134
  defined, 74
Achoui, M., 27
Ackerson, L. M., 86
Adams, G. R., 54
Adler, A., 100
Adolescents
  crystallizing identity and, 47
  different expectations for daughters, 134–136
  diffused, 54
  foreclosed, 54
  identity crisis of, 47, 54
  in immigrant families, 38–39, 133
  parenting styles and individuation of, 26–27, 53–56
  sexual development of, 89–90
  Western concepts of adolescence, 47, 48, 133
Al-Afghani, J., 20
Alarcon, R. D., 92
Al-Dahash, A. B., 53
Al-Haj, M., 13
Al-Issa, I., 88, 122–123, 138
Al-Jabiri, M. A., 12, 13, 17–18, 66, 72
Al-Khawaja, M. Y., 27
Al-Kittani, F., 53, 54
Alldredge, E. E., 126

Al-Mahroos, F., 53
Al-Masri, A. N., 53, 54
Alpha biases, x
Al-Sabaie, A., 89
Al-Shqerat, M. A., 53, 54
Al Tabari, 20
Al-Tahtawi, R. R., 20
Al-Tamimi, N. R., 29
Andalusia, 4
Anonymity, in the U.S., 36–37
Anorexia, 91–92
Anthrotherapy, 121–123
Anxiety, 83, 90
Anxiety disorders, 84–85
'Aql (mind or reason), 17, 19, 72
Arab-American Antidiscrimination Committee (ADC), 41, 42
Arab American Business and Profession Association (AABPA), 42
Arab American Institute (AAI), 29, 42
Arab American Medical Association (AAMA), 42
Arab-Americans. *See also* Arab/Muslim immigrants to the U.S.
  Arab organizations for, 41–42
  concept of, 40
Arab Human Development Report (2002), 10
Arab/Muslim cultures, 12–28
  authoritarianism and, 5–6, 10–11, 25, 53–56
  authoritative value of language, 18
  collectivism and, 5–21
  compatibility and deviation with, 8–11
  demographics of, 5, 10–11
  exposure to Western culture, 21–24
  family structure in, 24–28
  gender roles in, 13, 24–28
  history and, 3–5
  imagination and metaphor in, 138–139
  impact of September 11, 2001 terrorist attacks on perceptions of, x

About the Author

Marwan Dwairy is an associated professor of psychology at Emek Yezreel College and Oranim College. He is a licensed expert and supervisor in educational, medical, and developmental psychology. In addition, he is a licensed clinical psychologist. He received his B.A. and M.A. degrees in psychology from Haifa University, and his D.Sc. from the Faculty of Medicine at the Technion in 1991. In 1978 he established Israel's first psychological services center for Arabs in Nazareth, Israel. He continues to serve in his capacity as a supervisor in different psychological centers. Dr. Dwairy has developed and standardized several psychological tests for Arabs. He is also a reviewer for several journals and has served on the editorial board of *Clinical Psychology Review*, editing a special issue (December 1999) for that journal devoted to cross-cultural psychotherapy in the Middle East. He has published several books and articles on cross-cultural psychology and mental health among Arabs in which he presented his models and theories concerning culturally sensitive psychology. Dr. Dwairy can be emailed at psy@marwandwairy.com and his website found at www.marwandwairy.com.